N t

222

The guidebook that covers every square mile of the New Forest

By Jodi Longyear

Illustrations by Carina Krause

Published by Hammond's Green Publications

ISBN 978-1-8382797-0-7

Printed and bound by
Short Run Press Ltd, Exeter, Devon

Foreword

The initial inspiration for *New Forest 222* came from a delightful book named *Dartmoor 365* by Dartmoor aficionado John Hayward. I have owned a copy for over a decade and it is always in my bag when I take a trip to Devon. The premise for the title is that Dartmoor National Park covers (or covered) 365 square miles: one square mile for each day of the year. John Hayward overlaid Dartmoor with a square mile grid and wrote about a highlight in each square.

One gloomy December I spend two days tramping through the worst weather Dartmoor could throw at me. I travelled from the eastern edge of the moor to the Warren House Inn, near the centre. After drying my gear in the pub I set up a tent not far away, before returning to the edge of the moor by a different route the next day. This trip took in 22 'highlights' including reservoirs, a prehistoric pound and some amusingly shaped rocks. Back home, the following day, I walked in brilliant sunshine into the New Forest and visited some sights I had never seen, even though they were so close to my doorstep. I thought to myself, 'There needs to be a New Forest version of Dartmoor 365.' And now there is.

Acknowledgements

Lots of people have been instrumental in helping me make this book happen. Ian Coppack, Louisa Mason and Jon Triggs spent many days with me as fellow Duke of Edinburgh Award instructors in the New Forest; Ian introduced me to *Dartmoor 365*. Carina Krause has produced exactly the kind of drawings I wanted for the book. Fran Royle has made me smile with her kind comments as she has edited my sometimes wildly wayward words. Carpenter and explorer Ben Willis has been my go-to person for tips on trees. Liz Collins has been my map expert throughout the project and created the tick box maps for me. The design team of Paul Luffman and Glen Padgham of Short Run Press Ltd helped turn my rough plans into reality. Special thanks to Sue Mansbridge and Phil Murphy for letting me use their extraordinary photographs. Thanks also to Adge Cutler for allowing me to use his words, and Rob Hayward for letting me use his father's words – I couldn't have said it half as well. Many people have guided me on New Forest flowers, including Tom Starks, Sue Woodford and Clare Johnson. For nearly two years, Paul Wraight has listened patiently to my updates and tales on a weekly basis.

Friends who have offered encouragement, support and ideas include Alex Hoyle, Ally Hayes, Al Palmer, Wendy Stokes, Rikki Crossley, Paul Webb, among many others. Thank you also to Vincent, Cesar and Calvin for 'enduring' numerous trips to the far-flung corners of the New Forest and to Michelle Byrne for her patience as I visited, obsessed and wrote about my outdoor home.

Many thanks also to the Ordnance Survey for producing such fantastic maps. I have lost count of the hours (days) that I have spent poring over the map to find points of interest and oddities that needed investigating. Any errors or omissions are entirely mine.

Introduction

How to use this guidebook

There are no hard and fast rules – it is your guidebook and you can use it however you wish. The most important thing is that you use it! Although the idea of a 222-square-mile grid overlaid on the National Grid implies a strict sense of order, you will soon notice that I have bent the rules. There are several highlights which sit just outside their square or the New Forest boundary.

There is also the question of how big the New Forest is. The first three sources found by Google in September 2020 list it as 218, 219 and 220 square miles. I settled on 222 as this figure includes the two areas excluded, following court cases, from the final National Park. Both Fawley Power Station and Hinton Admiral Estate were removed at the owners' requests. Additionally, I thought 222 has a nice shape and sound to it.

Regarding flexible rules, if you do not see a fox on Fox Hill, do not be disappointed, neither did I. Visiting Fox Hill and then seeing a fox anywhere else in the New Forest is just as good! Some areas are best visited in certain seasons, but any visit is better than no visit. An enjoyable three-hour walk in the New Forest during which you fail to find any of the highlights in the book is a great success nonetheless.

Maps and navigation

217 of the squares in this book can be found on Ordnance Survey's (OS) 1:25,000 Explorer OL22 New Forest map. Frustratingly, five squares (T6–8 and U7–8) are missing. This is partly due to the New Forest's expansion northwards, when it was designated a National Park. Ordnance Survey have produced updated maps to reflect the new boundary, but as maps are a standard size they have not yet worked out how to include these 'northern outposts'. OS Explorer OL131 (Andover) includes the missing squares. I am a big fan of paper maps and heartily recommend buying one to get full enjoyment out of the New Forest. However, the New Forest is not a dangerous place without a map in the way that Dartmoor or Snowdonia would be. If you're prepared to get lost or get wet feet you could visit all 222 sites without a paper map.

If your schooldays are a distant haze and you are not sure how to use six-figure grid references there are some great video resources to remind you. Steve Blackshall and Ordnance Survey have put together several videos on all aspects of maps. Video 5 in the series (www.youtube.com/watch?v=FXuo_ocVMVU) explains what to do in just two minutes. As a bonus it also explains how to get to the church in square Q9.

Many of us use technology to navigate and there are a myriad of options. One of the best is to buy a paper map which comes with a free mobile download, allowing you to access OS Explorer OL22 on your phone so you know exactly where you are. Bear in mind that your phone mapping is only as good as your battery!

Free mapping on your phone is also very accessible. This website – https://osmaps.ordnancesurvey.co.uk – allows you to type in the grid reference you are searching for as well as showing your position. Simply type the full grid reference mentioned in the book (e.g. SU 232141) into the 'Search for location' box. This will take you to within 100m^2 of your objective. The description and a little investigation should enable you to find what you are looking for.

Googlemaps

If you want help getting to the location from your home you might find Google Maps (www.google.co.uk/maps) useful. Unfortunately Google Maps does not use grid references, but the Ordnance Survey website will give you the information you need, using the following process.

- First type the full grid reference mentioned in the book (e.g. SU 185140) into the 'Search for location' box at https://osmaps.ordnancesurvey.co.uk.
- Then click on 'More info' in the dialogue box next to the dropped pin.
- This reveals the latitude and longitude in a box on the left of the screen.
- Copy and paste the latitude and longitude into the Google Maps search box at www.google.co.uk/maps in the following format: 50° 55′ 30″ N 1° 44′ 17″ W.
- This will give you a route to a point close to where you will want to go. Beware of following Google Maps too uncritically as it can take you down private roads/impassable tracks close to your objective.

Environment and nature

One of the most distressing lessons of the summer 2020 lockdown was that some people had no idea how to treat nature. From people defecating on Dorset beaches, to dumping all their camping equipment in the Lake District, to setting fire to heathland with portable barbecues, the stories made grim reading. I am sure no one who buys this guidebook would dream of behaving in such a way, but it would be remiss of me not to mention both obvious and not-so-obvious guidelines for protecting the environment.

All litter should be taken home. The New Forest is a rural area and the few litter bins are quickly overwhelmed; then they are targeted by ponies and foxes. The saying 'Take nothing but photographs and leave nothing but footprints' is the rule here. This includes 'natural litter' such as banana peel, which can take up to two years to decompose and is not native food for any forest creatures. Many people go a step further and try to collect at least one piece of litter on their visit, thus making a positive contribution. A particular type of litter which is most unwelcome in the New Forest is the disposable barbecue. These have caused a number of fires and people are asked not to use them anywhere in the forest. Forestry England run a number of barbecue sites which can be booked and campsites often have barbecue areas.

Much of the New Forest is quite resilient to footprints, horses' hooves and bicycle tyres; however some paths are very quick to erode. These should be avoided if possible, especially if a nearby gravel path would suffice. When you do need to use an eroded path it is generally better to continue on the original line rather than skirt it, creating a path as wide as a motorway.

Animals mostly ignore people in the New Forest, perhaps puzzled that we are not eating grass or worms like they are. However, this changes during the breeding season and when they are raising their young. Cows, ponies and pigs can be very protective of their young and are often found in the open forest. If you have ever met a feisty sow you will know to steer clear. When crossing farmland during lambing season it is important to limit disturbance of ewes and their young. Ground-nesting birds are much more difficult to spot, but the areas of heathland where they rear their young are generally signposted by the Forestry Commission. Some are best completely avoided, and sometimes nearby car parks are closed. In other areas keeping dogs on a lead and sticking to footpaths will suffice.

Picking wild flowers is antisocial, and – if you should chance upon any that are rare or endangered – it is illegal. It is certainly illegal to uproot any wild flowers – best leave them where they are for others to enjoy. It is not illegal to pick mushrooms and other fungi for your own use, but it is a problem when commercial operators clear whole areas of mushrooms, damaging the ecosystem – report it if you see it. Identifying both flowers and mushrooms can provide hours of entertainment on a walk, but it can only be done if the visitor before you hasn't picked everything!

Transport

The New Forest is a beautiful but fragile environment so the fewer fumes we bring into it the better. However, for some people travelling by car is the only viable option for visiting and there are plenty of car parks to cater for them. Unfortunately there are also lots of peak season and weekend traffic jams, both in car parks and on the road. This guidebook does cover every corner of the New Forest, allowing you to avoid Lyndhurst on an August weekend. Electric vehicle charging facilities are slowly improving and most of the larger tourist attractions, as well as Hampshire County Council car parks, have charging stations.

Many squares are easily accessed from the London-Wareham main train line. Nearly 40 squares are within one mile of a train station. In the north of the New Forest, West Dean station offers great longer walks to squares U7 and U8. Bikes can be carried on most trains and offer a chance to visit a much larger area. Many of the cycle paths in the New Forest are top quality and allow you to escape into the heart of the forest.

Buses criss-cross the New Forest and get you to some of the places the train has stopped serving. In the summer there are three different open-top bus routes covering most of the New Forest. These are very good value for people who are planning several days of excursions. If you're lucky the weather will be nice!

If you are based in Southampton or the Isle of Wight the ferry is your gateway to the New Forest. There is probably no better way to view the New Forest than from the Solent, so this is great for a lucky few.

Respect

You will notice that there are many information signs beside roads and car parks across the New Forest. These signs are put up in order to protect the environment and animals. With 222 square miles of heathland, forest and coast to visit it is really quite easy to change your plans if a sign asks you not to enter an area – for instance, where ground-nesting birds are incubating eggs or rearing chicks. Signs asking people to refrain from feeding ponies are there because this has caused problems in the past – ponies have eaten the wrong type of food, or – having been fed by tourists in the past – have come to expect food and become aggressive.

Accidents involving ponies and deer are all too common across the New Forest. The 40mph speed limit in the open forest is primarily in place to reduce collisions between vehicles and animals. High-risk areas often have warning signs as well. Donkeys are particularly adept at playing 'chicken' with motorists, a game which no one wins.

Inconsiderate parking is generally only a problem during summer weekends. Parking on verges can damage drainage channels and create blind spots for drivers. Blocking lanes and entrances causes massive annoyance to locals and visitors alike. Thousands of people work in the New Forest, and agricultural machinery in particular has difficulty squeezing past poorly parked vehicles.

There are hundreds of miles of right of way in and around the New Forest. Many of these cross farmland and most farmers are very good at preserving access. If there are issues they should be addressed via Hampshire County Council (or Wiltshire in the very north of the area). Alongside this amazing right, we also have a responsibility to the communities that live and work in the area. Most of the things we should do are covered by common sense and courtesy and are probably best summed up by the very practical Scottish Outdoor Access Code's three key principles:

- Respect the interests of others.
- Care for the environment.
- Take responsibility for your own actions.

Shop local

The New Forest has a large farming community producing a wide range of foodstuffs including honey, beer, strawberries, flour, pumpkins and a whole lot more. Many of these can be bought in local towns and villages as well as farm shops. Sampling local produce is far more interesting than bringing in supermarket products and can turn a picnic into the highlight of the day.

Many local pubs and restaurants also specialise in locally-sourced food and drink. There are too many to list here, but some are mentioned in the main text. Finding a good eatery can be just as exciting as finding a boundary stone or a Japanese cedar! In our increasingly homogenised world, eating local is a treat and the New Forest is a great place to do it.

Dogs

Many people believe that there is no point going for a walk unless you take a dog. It is a very popular activity in the New Forest and in most areas dogs are welcome throughout the year. Unfortunately, dogs' inquisitive nature means they do not mix well with ground-nesting birds. These birds are vulnerable from March to July, so in heathland areas dogs should be kept on leads or the areas avoided entirely. The same advice applies to nature reserves. Most affected areas display signs to advise dog walkers when ground-nesting birds are at risk. Further advice can be found on the New Forest National Park Authority website under 'Dog walking code'. Finally, the most obnoxious litter to be found in the New Forest is dog poo bags, often hanging in trees. Words fail me . . .

Map 1

This map gives you an idea of where the main villages, roads and railways are. This will help you navigate the book.

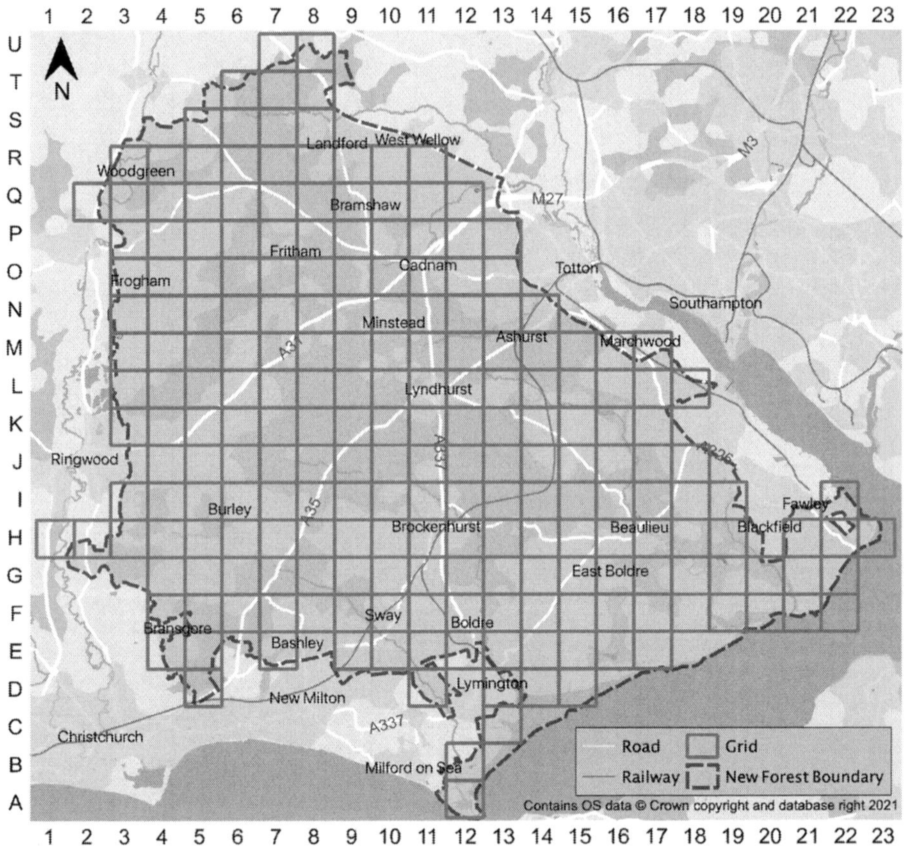

Map 2

This map is intended for those people (like me) who like ticking things off. Alternatively, you can colour the squares, cross them out or simply ignore them.

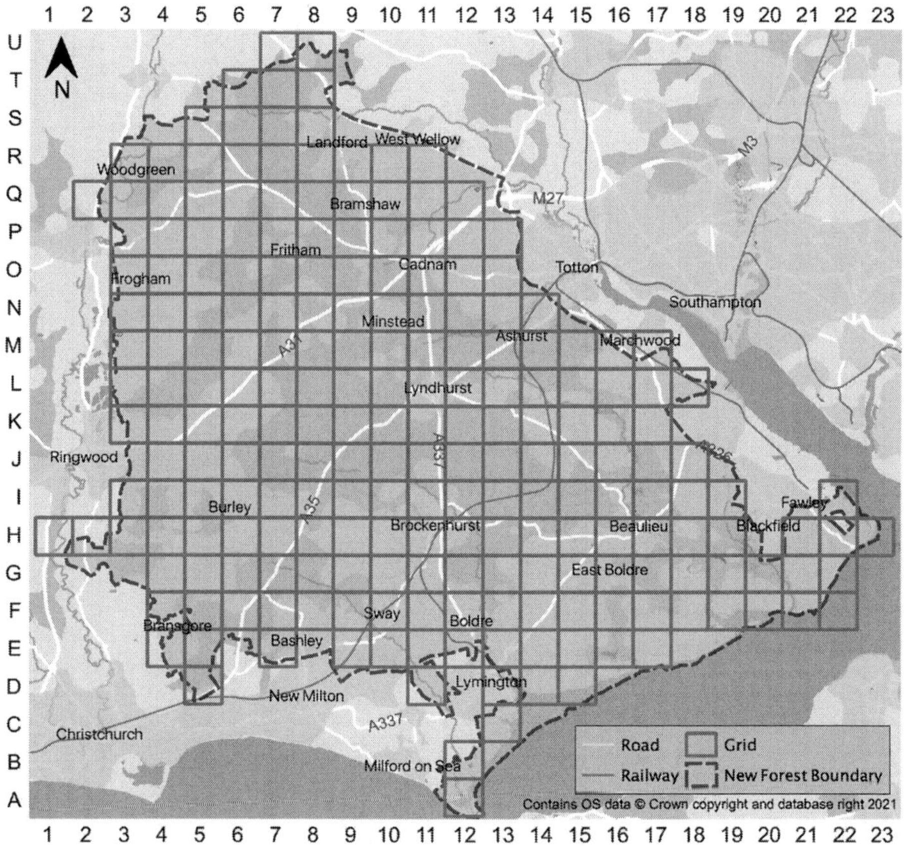

A12 Hurst Spit

GR SZ 318899

Whether it's the roar of ocean breakers or the pitter-patter splash of waves whipped up by the wings of herring gulls, the call of the sea will impel you over the crest of Hurst Spit. You can walk 30 metres from the lagoon (or lakes) to the Channel or 3,000 metres from Milford on Sea to Hurst Castle; both will be pleasant journeys.

Conditions can be different each day, so check that the forecast matches your mood. On 25 December 2019, for example, the weather was sunny, the wind light, and hordes of people perambulated back and forth. Some summer days bring out swimmers and sun worshippers whereas a winter storm threatens the very existence of the spit and the castle.

Many will be content to enjoy the beach and the sea with the views across to the Isle of Wight and back to Keyhaven. If you visit Hurst Castle there is even more to see. It was started during the reign of Henry VIII in 1541 and was in use for over 400 years, including both World Wars. You can pay to visit the castle (a worthwhile trip) or just enjoy the outside. Interesting features include the narrow-gauge railway used to transport supplies to the castle and the castle's two lighthouse towers.

On the castle's western flank are large chunks of eroded masonry, resembling glacial erratic boulders, abandoned on the shore. These huge chunks of brickwork are a warning of what might happen to the castle without coastal protection. Just behind the castle is Hurst Point Lighthouse, worthy of a visit by itself. The history of the three lighthouses is displayed in the castle.

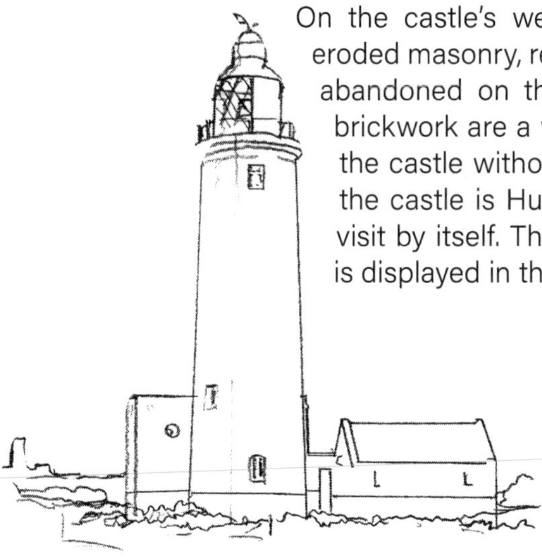

B12 Keyhaven

GR SZ 305915

Keyhaven is a hamlet nestling behind Hurst Castle Spit. Keyhaven was mentioned as a port as far back as 1026 and fishing was an important industry until quite recently. A glance across Keyhaven marshes shows that tourism, in the form of boating, is now the key industry. Any spare land or accessible water seems to have a boat on it. At high tide the lines of boats are puzzling but low tide reveals the 'lakes' where they continue to float.

The mudflats are very important for birds and link to the nearby Keyhaven Marshes. The formation of these salt marshes is due their protection by Hurst Beach. Views from Keyhaven are stunning, with the marshes, spit, castle and the Needles on the Isle of Wight all visible in good weather.

North of Keyhaven lake and marshes is Avon Water. This is the smallest of the three rivers that flow through the New Forest and into the Solent. The OS map shows that some of the land here is below sea level, which is due to Avon Water meeting the sea via a balancing pond. The pond has a sluice gate to prevent seawater flooding inland at high tide. At low tide the gate allows the pond to empty and normal river flow to resume.

The Gun Inn in Keyhaven could have a page to itself – a visit is recommended.

C13 The Salterns

GR SZ 327937

In the 18th and 19th centuries this area was the source of much of Lymington's wealth and many of the fine buildings in the village date from that time. The Salterns were very different from what you see today. Between Lymington and Hurst Spit there were approximately 150 salt pans along with wind pumps and boiling houses. The quayside would have thronged with barges collecting the salt and taking it around the country and abroad.

The process was quite simple, though dirty and landscape-changing, and a similar system is still used in many countries today. Seawater was channelled into shallow pans, such as Eight Acre Pond, and the sun evaporated much of the water. Wind pumps then pumped the brine into coal-powered boiling houses where the rest of the water was evaporated.

At one stage Lymington was the most important salt-producing region in the country. The glory days continued until 1865 when the Cheshire salt towns finally gained pre-eminence. The area around Northwich had been mined for salt since Roman times, but the arrival of the canals meant Cheshire salt became cheaper than Lymington salt.

The area is now part of a nature reserve, and birds and tourists have taken the place of salt workers. It's hard to imagine the scene here in the early 1800s but the St Barbe Museum in Lymington has a lot of interesting additional information.

D5 The trials and tribulations of Hinton Admiral Station

GR SZ 202948

Hinton Admiral Station has every reason to feel sorry for itself. Opened in 1888 on the prestigious London to Bournemouth line, it was named Hinton Station after the nearby hamlet. However, it was soon realised that nobody knew where Hinton was; on the OS map, even today, the word Hinton sits in a field with just a few houses within 500 metres. After less than two months the station was renamed Hinton Admiral for Highcliffe-on-Sea. This better reflected reality, as the Meyrick family's country estate of Hinton Admiral was well known and Highcliffe-on-Sea was a growing town.

Things ticked along nicely for the station until April Fool's Day, 1974, when the Local Government Act transferred Highcliffe, Burton, Christchurch and Bournemouth from Hampshire to Dorset. The new county boundary, between the River Mude and Walkford Brook, was formed by the railway line, so politicians were faced with either linking the station with Highcliffe in Dorset, the source of the majority of its passengers, or keeping its historic links with the Tapps-Gervis-Meyrick baronetcy in Hampshire. Needless to say, they went for Hinton Admiral in Hampshire! So Hinton Admiral Station forms a small Hampshire island in Dorset.

Misnamed after a place no one knew, rejected by Dorset, renamed again; there was one final insult in store. On 1 April 2005 the New Forest National Park came into existence, and its border sits just 200 metres north of the station. Though rejected by the New Forest and in need of a lick of paint, Hinton Admiral Station has made it into *New Forest 222*!

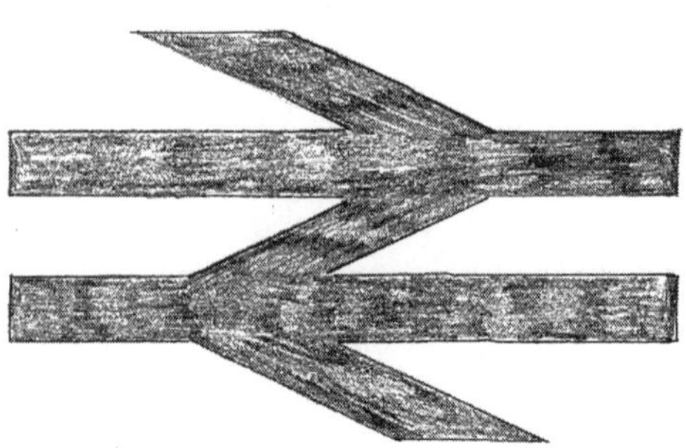

D11 Upper Pennington Common

GR SZ 299954

Upper Pennington Common, starting a few hundred metres to the west of its more civilised neighbour Pennington Common, is a wild place. If you want to walk your dog or take the children to a play park, or you have forgotten your boots then Pennington Common (GR SZ 305953) is a better idea. The southernmost part is essentially a riot of trees on an acid bog. The right of way is pretty much the only area you have access to and any trees that fall or are felled are left beside the 'path'. If you try to venture away from the path you will end up very wet, dirty and smelly.

The northern part of the Common provides access to Avon Water. This is the only place you can visit this clear-running stream between the New Forest perambulation (boundary) and Keyhaven at the sea. Stiles allow access to the boggy area of grass and then the boggy woodland. Beside the stream is just a narrow muddy track with various offshoots disappearing into the surrounding woods. It is quite an adventure compared to the typical New Forest gravel paths and there are plenty of opportunities to trip or slip into Avon Water!

To conclude:

- Pennington Common for clean and gentle fun or promenading.
- Upper Pennington Common for dirty thrills and potential spills.

D13 Lymington's monument to its local hero

GR SZ 332958

'Welcome to the Burrard Monument – one of Britain's finest obelisks.' The information boards tell you everything you need to know about this monument, tucked away beside a minor road and missed by most visitors. The monument was erected in 1840, following the death of long-term MP, Admiral Sir Harry Burrard Neale. From the coast just south of the monument, a short train ride will take you into Lymington with its delightful and relaxing waterfront area.

Lymington Pier train station is a relic from the days of train ferries. A ten-carriage train used to travel from London to the Isle of Wight up until the 1960s. In modern times this has been replaced by a branch-line train that requires a short walk to the ferry and, since trains have all but disappeared on the Isle of Wight, some other mode of transport when you get there.

A single 1st class ticket from Lymington Pier to Lymington might seem a snip at £4.20 (2020 prices). However further investigation would reveal the journey length to be only 666 metres – over £6 per kilometre. This would translate into a Lymington Pier to Waterloo ticket of almost £1000! Timewise, the journey takes two minutes, at a grand average speed of 20kph. At that speed, London would be eight hours away.

If you still want to catch the train into Lymington you can save cash by buying a £2.60 2nd class ticket. There is also the option of walking into Lymington via the causeway, which is a perfectly pleasant stroll.

D14 Boldre Foreshore Nature Reserve

GR SZ 347950

Less than a kilometre from the hustle and bustle of Lymington is the start of Boldre Foreshore Nature Reserve. Access to the shore can be gained via a right of way starting at the end of Shotts Lane. At high tide you might find the sea lapping at the end of the track, with no chance of getting onto the shore. At these times a permissive footpath starting at GR SZ 345952 gives access to the fields running parallel to the coast and the large coastal pond south of Pylewell House.

At low tide the nature reserve announces itself with a cawing cacophony. Sea birds tend not to possess the sweet song of many land birds so the noise can be jarring. However the area is a twitcher's dream, with a wonderful selection of birds enjoying the seaside buffet that mud flats provide. Summer visitors include lapwings, ringed plover, gulls and terns. In the winter you can expect to see brent geese, wigeon, dunlins, curlews, redshanks and, if you are lucky, even a goosander.

Another unusual visitor to the shore is the New Forest pony. Despite having access to a whole forest full of vegetation, ponies often venture down to the shore to sample the slightly saltier variety available here.

If all this talk of food has left you craving your picnic there are two good spots nearby. The shore at the end of Tanners Lane (GR SZ 364953) is quite wide and high enough not to be covered in seaweed. If you prefer to get away from the shore, there is a lovely spot next to the cricket ground on the Pylewell Estate (GR SZ 354962).

D15 Gnarled oaks

GR SZ 359952

I am certain that, when compiling the *Oxford English Dictionary*, a researcher visited this exact corner of the New Forest. It is quite special as it is one of the only areas where deciduous woodland meets the sea. Any cliff on this stretch of coast is measured in centimetres rather than metres, so the trees grow right on the beach.

These oaks have been shaped by their position on the coast. Though protected by the mud flats of Boldre Foreshore, waves have still exposed large sections of their root systems. Prevailing south-westerly winds have twisted them into travesties of branches and trunks. In places the remains of wooden revetments sit uselessly in front of the trees and shoreline they were meant to protect – a kind of visual ironic juxtaposition.

> '**gnarled** *adjective* knobbly, rough, and twisted, especially with age: *the gnarled old oak tree*.'

Plummers Water, one source of which you may have visited in square F14, reaches the coast near this point. At the mouth of the stream is a bridge protected by what could easily be described as very gnarled sea defences. Rough, lumpy concrete chunks with twisted mooring bollards still attached are protected by vertical railway sleepers driven into the sea bed. Is this a coincidence or a case of nature inspiring humankind?

E4 The edge of Dorset

GR SZ 183965

In one way this is a square for the map geeks, but successfully finding the edge of Dorset means you've walked through some delightful farmland scenery. There are multiple routes from Bransgore, the Avon or even the coast.

For just over a kilometre, between Harrow Road in the north and Waterditch Road in the south, the boundary of the New Forest coincides with the boundary of Dorset. There is only one footpath that crosses the boundary, a place where you can safely have one foot in a National Park and one foot in the West Country.

On the map the boundary is a complicated line: there is the blue line indicating the River Mude with the dot-dash line of a county boundary running along it. To the east is the pink dashed line showing the edge of the New Forest and to the west a fence or similar boundary (in this case a large hedgerow and trees). Running parallel for a short distance before crossing the Mude is a black dashed footpath and a green dashed right of way, which are one and the same.

The footpath crosses on an unmarked footbridge, which you'll be grateful for, as the Mude is wide enough here to offer a challenge. You will now be either entering or leaving the New Forest, and Hampshire, and Dorset. I hope you enjoyed your stay.

E5 The remains of Tin Town and the story of those who lived there

GR SZ 203977, 198973

Part of the story of Tin Town has been told elsewhere (F6). However, at the grid references above remains of hut bases are still visible on the edge of Harrow Wood. Adge Cutler, former resident and authority on Tin Town, has very kindly given permission for me to include these insights into life in these huts from his website:

'My father always said this was a terrible place to live with all the hardships all the families had to put up with. However, I must say that my own memories where only good ones being a young kid.'

'My dad had to do the shopping on the way home from his work at MEXE, Barrack Road, Christchurch, otherwise it was a long walk to Bransgore and back, where the only shop was, especially in winter time along cold dark lanes. Very few people had transport which in those days was mainly a bicycle.'

'My father was told by Christchurch Town Council we would be at Holmsley for up to two years, and in the Nissen hut we had running water, electric light and a cooking range. Rent was 12 shillings and sixpence a week which included electricity. In today's decimal currency this equals 62 and a half pence; converted to 2017 values is £72.36 a week!'

'There were no flush toilets only forerunners of the Portaloo which were emptied at communal toilets. To bathe, out came the tin bath in front of the fire or washing in an enamel bowl. Rationing ended when I was four years old. Dad always said he needed a torch or candles as the lights would often go out. I remember collecting fir cones and wood with my father to keep the range alight.'

'The downside to summer was that because the huts were surrounded by trees and bushes there were quite a lot of flies about during the daytime, also the huts got hot and stuffy. Icy cold during the winter.'

'No television as these were very, very expensive, and we only had a big radio.'

(http://lcars.org.uk/Holmsley.htm)

E7 Sammy Miller's eclectic Motorcycle Museum

GR SZ 231962

One of the more unusual sights featured in this book is a two-seater plane itching to take off outside a classic square courtyard of a manor farm. This is the first indication that the Sammy Miller Motorcycle Museum is far more than a simple museum of motorcycles.

Surrounding the building are items of farming paraphernalia sitting together with a statue of a stag and the aforementioned aircraft. Alpacas, donkeys, goats and budgerigars are amongst the animals you will see on your way into the courtyard. The courtyard contains shops and a café as well as a knife sharpening trailer, cannons and other items of interest.

But none of this wonderful stuff quite prepares you for the inside of the building, which is jam packed with motorcycles. The museum is dedicated to motorbikes and a tribute to its founder Sammy Miller MBE, an 11 times British Champion with hundreds of accolades and trophies, many of which are on display. However, it is also much more than that: there are weapons, sewing machines, adverts, instruments and so much more. The museum is a celebration of engineering and design of so many types and everyone will find things of interest. Rather than trying to pick your favourite item in the museum, you will probably need to choose your top ten.

Described as a living museum, as almost every motorbike is in running order (even if some are over a century old), you will often get a chance to see or chat to Sammy himself. The convivial Ulsterman is as enthusiastic about motorbikes today as he was when he started his racing career as a teenager. You can visit the site for free, but I highly recommend the museum as well. You do not need to be a petrolhead to enjoy it as there is literally something for everyone – you just have to find it!

E9 Tiptoe Garage

GR SZ 256977

Tiptoe Garage is a delightful throwback to the 1960s. The building itself could have been designed by a child with its simple, symmetrical lines. 'TIPTOE GARAGE' has been painted in striking red capitals in a neat curve that resembles the lower roofline of the Rising Sun pub in Wootton.

The pièce de résistance is the clock. Just below the apex of the roof, in the centre of the building and the sign, the clock is a true centrepiece. Look closely and you will observe that the numbers have been replaced with letters, spelling TIPTOE GARAGE. The 'P' is at 12 o'clock, so 12.15 would be E past P. Due to the duplication of letters telling 'Tiptoe Time' soon becomes very complicated.

Less complicated are the Tiptoe facts below:

Tiptoe – apparently derived from the French surname 'Typetot'

In-between parishes – part of Tiptoe is in Sway and part in Hordle

Post Office – used to be housed next to the garage but closed in 2008

Tiptoe – a funny name for a village, but so is Sway if you think about it

One hundred residents – Tiptoe has slightly less than 100, but two churches!

Edge of the New Forest – Tiptoe is on a strip of land between the actual forest and the park boundary

Garage – from the French word 'garer', meaning to shelter

Avon Water – flows past Tiptoe. Avon is the old English word for river so it means 'River Water'

Railway – the London-Weymouth line passes Tiptoe, with the nearest station one mile away in Sway

Arnewood Common – part of Tiptoe but neither common land, nor wooded, nor belonging to Arne

Garage – a type of music made famous in 1999 by Artful Dodger and Craig David from Southampton

End – that's enough Tiptoe facts.

E10 Sway Tower

GR SZ 279967

South of the small village of Sway is one of the most unusual buildings in the New Forest. Presiding over the collection of family homes, bungalows and farms in this rural area is Peterson's Folly. The Forest area has many follies but none quite match the folly built for High Court judge Andrew Peterson in the 1880s.

At 70 metres and 14 floors high this is the tallest building in the New Forest. It is also the tallest building in the world to be made of non-reinforced concrete, though whether that is a recommendation is questionable. The basic square design of the tower has a 330-step hexagonal staircase allowing access to the 13 individual rooms that sit above the larger ground floor.

The views from the top must be stunning, with the New Forest to the north and the Solent to the south. The tower has previously housed a hotel and restaurant but is currently privately owned.

What Judge Peterson was thinking when he came up with the idea of his folly is unknown. What is known is that local workers and products (such as Portland cement) were utilised to create a building that still inspires awe 140 years later.

E11 Gordleton's old mill

GR SZ 292961

The area around the interestingly-named hamlet of Bowling Green is full of nurseries and stables. Footpaths criss-cross the area but do not reach the centre of the hamlet where The Wheel Pub, the New Forest's only community-owned pub, sits empty, apparently permanently, a victim of Covid-19. If you head west along Silver Street pub-based disappointment turns into curiosity and then amazement as you discover The Mill at Gordleton.

This seventeenth-century water mill has been transformed into a beautiful place for eating, drinking, sleeping or even just visiting to admire. Many old mills have become private dwellings so it is nice to be able to explore an accessible example.

Outside, the building is attractively clad in foliage. Beside it runs Avon Water, the New Forest's 'third' river, in fine fettle here. This waterway was subdivided and diverted to power the original mill and numerous bridges allow you to view the river. In fine weather this is an ideal spot to sit next to the river, sheltered by a willow tree and taking on board a refreshing drink. The beer garden and waterside terrace are surrounded by trees, chiefly the willows and eucalyptus.

The garden doubles as an art display with sculpted rocks, life-size terminators and metal arachnids on show amongst countless other pieces. There is a carp pond and numerous areas to explore as well as chairs and benches. Indoors the building is fascinating, with artefacts museums would be proud to display.

The Mill at Gordleton has many charms, most of which are natural and timeless and well worth stopping for.

E12 Buckland Rings (old Lymington)

GR SZ 315968

Its fertile soil and access to fresh water made Lymington a good choice for a settlement during the Iron Age, long before yachts and Range Rovers had been imagined. The Iron Age site is at Buckland Hill, just north of present-day Lymington. Too little has been excavated to allow accurate dating, but in the British Isles the Iron Age lasted from 800 BC–AD 100, so the sculpted earth banks and ditches are likely to have been in place for over 2,000 years. What is known is that the Buckland Rings site was a defensive hill fort built to protect a farming community. Farming would have taken place all around the fort, to which people retreated in times of danger.

Buckland Rings has three layers of banks separated by two large ditches. On three sides of the rectangular site these are comparatively well preserved, with the north and south sides covered by ancient woodland. The eastern flank was partially levelled for farming in quite modern times; the whole fort site was under cultivation into the 1980s. Now under the enlightened ownership of Hampshire County Council, the Rings and the field to the south are protected and preserved for nature and learning. There are numerous information boards across the site, including a 3-D model on the raised ground south of Buckland Rings.

In the past, less enlightened ownership allowed two houses to be built on the western side of the site. Planning laws must have been very lax to allow houses to be built on the site of a 2,000-year-old fort. Houses aside, Buckland Rings is a beautiful place to enjoy the views and nature, to scramble around, to picnic or to play football. After all, people have been doing similar things here for millennia.

E13 Under the sea at zero metres?

GR SZ 321971

There are not many places on a map of the south coast where you can see the zero metres contour line. This is one such spot, despite being more than one kilometre from the tidal part of the Lymington River and twice that distance from the nearest waves.

To get to this spot you can either swim along the river (not recommended) or use a nearby public footpath. The northern route is more direct but less interesting. From the south you quickly get an impression of the lie of the land. After crossing the railway line, a '! Land Floods' sign greets you. Beyond this a long series of flood defences need to be first breached and then followed.

To the east, woodland quickly gives way to bog and although you cannot see the river you are nonetheless aware of it. The area teems with wildlife and birdsong fills the trees. There is an adder conservation area (entry not recommended). Though not the prettiest woodland, it supports a wonderful diversity of wildlife.

If you want to stand within the 0m contour ring then a stout stick, wellingtons, a GPS and a life jacket are all advisable. Alternatively you can look over the area, having enjoyed the journey to it and knowing that you've seen what it looks like below sea level.

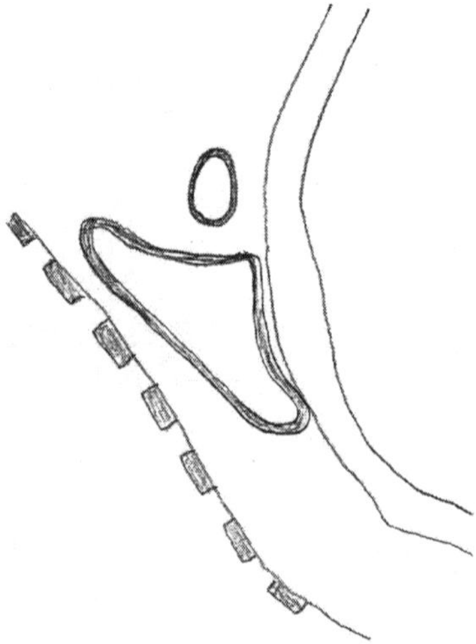

E14 RAF Lymington

GR SZ 343963

RAF Lymington was started in 1943, first used in 1944, closed in 1945 and returned to farmland in 1946. Somehow part of the site of the airfield has remained open and it is now the only place in the New Forest you can land a plane.

The original airfield had two runways: one ran north-south between Snooks and Shotts Lanes; the second south of and parallel to South Baddesley Road. The former runway is the one that is in use today though it is less than half its original length. The byway east of Snooks Farm gives a good view of the grass landing strip and one of the original blister hangars. These hangars were designed in 1939 as simple, portable buildings to store and maintain aircraft. It is unlikely anyone envisaged some would still be in use over 80 years later.

Signs on this byway advise you to look left and right before proceeding because any aircraft landing on the runway would be very low at this stage. At the junction with Shotts Lane are display boards and an example of the steel mesh used to reinforce the landing strips for the American Thunderbolts based here to support the D-Day landings.

The second runway ran straight across Pylewell Park. US officers were billeted in Pylewell House which must have been a better than average billet for the men stationed there. All hangars and hard standings, along with the runway, are long gone now; the only possible exception being a concrete and brick building 50 metres south of the publicly accessible war memorial. The building can be seen from the road and the public footpath but is close to neither so remains an enigma.

E15 The most romantic spot in Pylewell Park?

GR SZ 354961

Pylewell House is an impressive country house owned by Lord Teynham. The house and its park, laid out in 1890, have hosted many events – weddings, arts festivals and even a Dogstival (Testimonial: 'Pawfectly Executed!'

Public access is available all year round via a permissive footpath close to the coast and the Solent Way, which currently cuts straight across the park to the north of Pylewell House. Though public footpaths are not normally great places for picnics this is an exception. A delightful avenue of mature lime trees cuts between the cricket ground and Dod's Pond. If visiting in the spring, the trees will be exploding with new shoots and the ground will be carpeted with bluebells. Even the grass around the base of the trees seems luxuriant.

On a warm summer's day you could discreetly have the most quintessentially English picnic here, listening to the leather versus willow thwack of a cricket match, daintily nibbling cucumber sandwiches and washing them down with a thermos of tea whilst a gentle breeze wafts in the subtle salty aroma of the Solent. Enjoy.

E16 Sowley Pond

GR SZ 378966

On the map, Sowley Pond looks like a fantastic place to visit. Unfortunately there is no public access so only a glimpse of the pond is possible. The area has a fascinating history, summarised here:

Sowley Pond was built in the fourteenth century as a fishery by the monks of Beaulieu Abbey.

Oak trees make up much of the woodland around the pond.

Waterside woodland here once contained 60 pairs of heron – the largest number in Hampshire.

Long-distance footpath – the Solent Way passes within a few metres of Sowley Pond.

Earl of Southampton – established the ironworks here in the 1590s.

Ye Olde Ironworks – possibly the source of the railings and gate outside Sowley House.

Pond, Farm, House, Copse, Brooms, Marsh and Lane are all preceded by the word Sowley.

Origin of the stream that fills Sowley Pond – Two Bridges Bottom, a place with no bridges.

Naval orders allowed the ironworks to flourish here.

Damselflies (of the variable variety) have made this their only breeding site in the New Forest.

Fleet Pond claims to be the largest in Hampshire but is only 21 hectares compared to Sowley Pond's 47.

Abstraction from the pond and feeder streams is allowed but rarely impacts the water level.

Crockford Stream was dammed to create Sowley Pond.

'**T**he Sowley hammer can be heard' is said to be Forest-speak for 'Here comes the rain again'.

Sowley Estate used to be a part of the Beaulieu Estate but was sold off in the 1950s.

E17 Thorns Beach – the Hollywood of the New Forest

GR SZ 385974

There are plans afoot to reroute the Solent Way past the mansions of Thorns Beach. As it stands, though, there is no public access to this square other than driving or cycling along Sowley Lane (it is not really a nice walk). Instead, it is recommended you repair to the East End Arms (E15) or the beach at the end of Tanners Lane (D15) to try and work out which three famous people live in Thorns Beach. The crossword below gives you the words needed to complete a phrase revealing the answer.

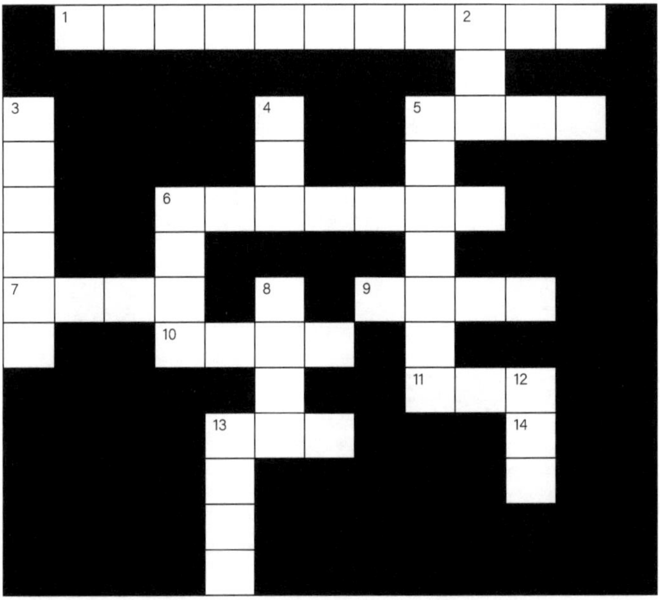

Add your answers to the boxes to spell out the phrase.

9 across	5 down	6 across	6 down	10 across	7 across
13 across	8 down	2 down	5 down	14 across	13 down
1 across	11 across	4 down	12 down	3 down	-

Across

1 Someone who is quite a bit richer than a millionaire (11)

5 Reed (of a loom) (4)

6 People who belong to an organisation (7)

7 The self-titled fourth album of German rapper Fler (4)

9 A word describing a bad situation (4)

10 An ornamental knob (4)

11 A male version of madam (3)

13 An important connecting word (3)

14 Same as 13 across (3)

Down

2 Feeling unwell (3)

3 An appropriately named high coastal village in Kent (6)

4 A shortened version of James (3)

5 Narrow areas of water (7)

6 To annotate (4)

8 An American term for a toilet (4)

12 The carrier of the fleas that spread the plague (3)

13 As well as (4)

If you have any answers – well done! The correct answers are on page 244 or you can Google 'Thorns Beach Residents' (if you haven't already).

F4 RAF Sopley/Airfields Heritage Centre

GR SZ 174979

Even if it wasn't painted two-tone green with a large sign saying 'FONFA New Forest Airfields Heritage Centre', this building would stand out as odd. The fact that a new housing estate has sprung up next to it only emphasises its singularity.

It's a square-cut military building typical of wartime austerity architecture. Built in the early 1940s to house a back-up generator for RAF Sopley, it passed into the hands of the Baily family who then kindly donated it to the Friends of the New Forest Airfields (FONFA). This is the last remaining building of the main camp at RAF Sopley, an early radar station which survived until 1974. RAF Winkton, a wartime Advanced Landing Ground, was also housed here to provide air support for the D-Day landings. The flat fields all around show why this area was chosen for RAF Winkton.

The opening times of the visitor centre are restricted to one Sunday a month at the time of writing which means an external view is all many will get. However there are many public footpaths through beautiful farmland which make the area a worthwhile visit. If you are lucky enough to get inside you will find yourself in the epicentre of New Forest military knowledge. Information is displayed everywhere and the volunteers are immensely knowledgeable and keen to help.

F5 Holmsley Gravel Pit Nature Reserve

GR SZ 207988

In the bad old days the Forestry Commission had a reputation for simply using the New Forest as a cash cow. This nature reserve is one of the longer-term unintended benefits of that strategy.

The pond that exists today is a result of years of extracting gravel to build forest tracks. Once the gravel pit closed it flooded and soon started to attract wildlife. Management of the site was passed to the Hampshire and Isle of Wight Wildlife Trust.

Though access is restricted it is possible to get a sighting of birds flying in and out as well as a slight view from the gate. Serious twitchers can also contact the Trust to ask permission to visit. There's a small area of bank in the southern corner which allows a view across both parts of the L-shaped water.

Many birds can be spotted here, depending on the time of year you come. Some of the easier ones to identify include:

- Grey heron – very tall (almost 1m long with a 2m wingspan. Grey, black and white feathers.
- Canada goose – large, grey body, white bib, black neck and face with a white stripe.
- Lapwing – black and white underneath with a greenish topside. Obvious punkish crest.
- Mallard – males are colourful with a green head, brown and grey body and yellow bill. Females often accompany the males and are brown with an orange bill.
- Teal – small ducks. Males have red and green heads and grey bodies. Females are brown.

F6 The New Forest Airfields Memorial

GR SZ 208987

A modern memorial, dedicated on the 16th August 2002, to 'commemorate the immense effort and sacrifices made in this area during the dark days of World War Two.' The Friends of the New Forest Airfields have constructed an austere and imposing memorial.

Many of the roads in this area are remnants of the roads in RAF Holmsley South, which covered this site from 1942–6. To the north of the monument areas of runway and taxiway are still intact and are used by locals for storage. The main use for the site is currently for camping - campsites either side of Forest Road use former aircraft hard standings for caravans and camper vans.

RAF Holmsley South supported both Operation Torch (the invasion of North Africa) and Operation Overlord (the invasion of Northern Europe). Many different types of aircraft took off here, from RAF Spitfires to USAAF B-24 Liberators. Lots more information can be found at the Friends of the New Forest Airfields Museum in square F4.

After the war the airfield was taken over by Christchurch Borough Council to create 'Tin Town' (also see square E5). The tin in question was the Nissen hut accommodation left by the RAF, which the council used to house families in the post-war housing shortage. Tin Town housed up to 400 people at a time when Brockenhurst had a population of only around 2,000. It was closed in 1961, so some people spent almost all of their childhood there - what an adventure!

F7 Boundary Post

GR SZ 227992

Nestling on a bank, next to a road and beside a wood is a little bit of administrative history represented by a concrete post.

Boundary posts (BP) are not uncommon in the New Forest, though boundary stones (BS) are far more common. Boundary stones tend to be much older and mark the boundaries of traditional manors. They can be difficult to find as soil, detritus and foliage build up over decades and slowly envelop them.

This boundary post is quite easy to spot as it projects around ½ metre out of the ground. It is a square concrete post with rounded edges and a cupola style top. First reading indicates 'GH OF LYMINGTON'. Further examination through the undergrowth and leaves show it reads 'BOROUGH OF LYMINGTON' – somewhat enlightening but no longer true.

The boundary here is currently between the parishes of Brockenhurst and New Milton. This has been the case since 1 April 1974 when the Borough of Lymington, in existence in some form from around 1200, was abolished. So this boundary post can be dated between 1932, when Lymington Borough was extended to include New Milton and three other modern parishes, and 1974.

Lymington should not feel too diminished by this loss of territory. The same Act of Parliament removed Bournemouth and Christchurch, plus a cricket ground the county team had been using since 1880, from Hampshire altogether.

F8 A tale of two watering holes

GR SZ 242983

A couple of hundred metres from the Rising Sun pub, beside the Holmsley Road, is a water trough. This is not particularly unusual in the New Forest but this trough has a mystery surrounding it. Carved in its stone side is an inscription which is rather hard to read, but appears to say: *'In memory of MRC, presented to the corporation of Brighton the jubilee year of Queen Victoria's reign by JEC 1887'.*

Exploration online finds a partial answer from a source of unknown reliability: 'I think you'll find the "M.R.C" is "M.R.G" and the "J.E.C" is "J.E.G". The JEG was a Miss J.E. Gordon of Woodlands, 28 St. John's Wood Road, N.W. who donated several troughs via the Metropolitan Drinking Fountain & Cattle Trough Association. This one was originally (from 1888) in Grand Parade Brighton. For some reason, that I have yet to find out (probably because Brighton Corporation wanted to get rid of all their cattle troughs), it was moved to the New Forest on 18th May 1948. I assume the M.R.G was Miss Gordon's father'

(https://derrickjknight.com).

Problem partially solved, so off to the Rising Sun in search of more mysteries and maybe some refreshment. On the facade of the pub, above the upper windows, the paintwork slightly resembles a rising sun. The windows are stained glass which can be dramatic, especially when the sun is rising or sinking. The pub has a public, private and hotel bar though they are all interchangeable these days. The decor is New Forest chic. There are paintings and photos of the Forest, especially its creatures, people and places including the gypsy culture, and many of the pub in slightly different iterations. The wallpaper in the back room is New Forest-esque though the religious building in the picture rather resembles the 123-metre spire of Salisbury Cathedral. Most mysterious is the time recorder in the snug. It is an amazing piece of kit that puts the woodsman's axe, milk churn and other items in the shade.

F9 Three bridges, three fords

GR SZ 264987

Avon Water has faced any number of attempts to straighten and 'improve' it over the centuries. This has mainly been done to try to drain the boggy land between Mead End and Holmsley Bog. As the OS map attests, most of these efforts have been in vain. Straight blue lines are surrounded by blue marsh symbols as nature shrugs off human efforts.

At this point the map shows the stream braided, with a straightened channel and an additional, more natural, channel. However just one footbridge is shown, suggesting anyone without wellington boots (strongly recommended) will face problems. On closer inspection there are four ways to cross the main channel and two for the more southerly one, excluding trees (more of that later).

The main channel is crossed by a ford, a footbridge and two large pipes. Clearly lots of adventurous people use the pipes –not recommended (though much more fun). The second channel just has two fords, suggesting it post-dates the bridge-building. This looks like another example of Avon Water disposing of man's proposals, as a bridge across half the stream seems rather pointless. Thankfully nature has provided some precarious crossing points – you can jump across narrow sections of stream, or use fallen trees if you're sure of your balance – good luck!

F10 Sway's Jubilee Oak

GR SZ 278982

Sway is a small village very much on the doorstep of the forest. To the north east is open heathland, there are woods to the north west, and to the south farmland. The village experienced a construction boom when the railway arrived in 1888 and many of the main buildings date from that period.

South of the centre, close to St Luke's Church, is a small, quiet traffic island with a prominent oak and a bench. This traffic island is called Jubilee Oak Green and on the end of the bench is a rusty plaque reading:

> *'This tree was planted in June 1897 to commemorate the Diamond Jubilee reign of Her Majesty Queen Victoria 1837 to 1897.'*

Though quite young for an oak, it is older than any person alive today. The oak was planted by local dignitaries the Revd Stephenson, Vicar of Sway, and Mr Herbert Moser, Chairman of the Parish Council.

The current bench was put in place 101 years after the tree and is the work of stonemason Martin Cook. It replaced a wooden one installed in 1935, to commemorate the jubilee of King George V and Queen Mary. Carved into it is the following prophecy:

> *'If you sit down here and whistle maybe a pony will come galloping from the darkest depths of the Forest into the village of Sway past the pub called the Crooked Cross all the way to this Jubilee Oak and if he lays his head on your knee you'll never go away.'*

The Crooked Cross pub has gone away and cattle grids thwart galloping ponies; however if you like Sway the bench is a nice place to sit and whistle.

The help of Katie Walding, Sway Parish Clerk, was invaluable in providing dates and names from the A-Z of Sway.

F11 Sailing in the New Forest

GR SZ 302990

Aside from the Solent coastline and Baron Montagu of Beaulieu's river, there are precious few opportunities to sail in the Forest. It is not really surprising – the clue is the word 'forest'. However, just as you can climb trees on Bikini Atoll in the Pacific, you can sail boats on Setley Pond in the New Forest. They just have to be small, ideally centimetres rather than metres. Setley Pond lies a kilometre south of the village it is named after. On the OS map, though, it is not named as such but as a tourist attraction: 'MODEL YACHT SAILING'.

Should you not have your own model yacht with you, there is a good chance someone else will be sailing theirs – it is a very popular spot. Dog walking, pony and bird watching, aqua-fetch for dogs and picnicking are also common activities here. Birds that commonly visit the pond include herons and cormorants, attracted by the presence of fish and absence of fishermen. During the Big Freeze of 1963 ice skating was even possible for a few months.

The pond itself varies in size depending on rainfall. Older maps (such as 2006) show just one pond but the 2020 version has a second, smaller pond to the north. During very wet periods one very large pond will form, flooding the car park in the process.

The Victorians had a big impact on the New Forest that we see today, so it should come as no surprise that during this period a gravel pit was dug here. However, the pond you see today is the result of wartime gravel extraction. If you should happen to see a model HMS *Hood* sailing on Setley Pond you should say a little thank-you to the sappers who dug it out in the 1940s.

F12 Perkins' Piece, Boldre

GR SZ 318984

Even the tiniest villages in the New Forest have interesting histories. Boldre, with a population of just a couple of hundred souls, has a lovely 15th century pub overlooking a village green with an interesting history. The green is called Perkins' Piece, and its history is explained on a noticeboard. The gist of the story is as follows.

Since the early 1700s the Jenvey family had run a thriving wheelwright's business from a cottage and forge on the site. However, the growth of motor transport around the time of the Second World War spelled the end of the wheelwright's trade and the buildings here fell into ruin and were demolished. During the war the thatch on a nearby cottage caught fire and it had to be demolished, leaving an area of open grass.

In 1951 the site was bought by John Perkins, OBE, of Boldre Bridge House, Chairman of the *Southampton Daily Echo*. He had intended to build two houses on it; but planning permission was refused and in 1977 he decided to give the land to Boldre Parish. He arrived for the handover ceremony driving a pony and trap, and the green was named in his honour.

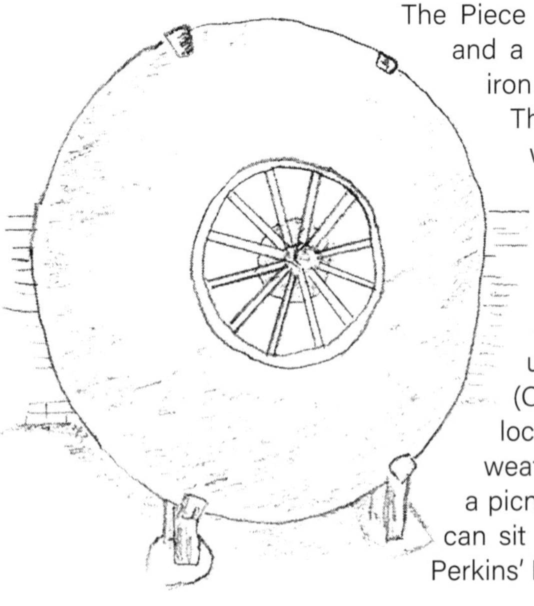

The Piece has two benches, two bins and a post box as well as a large iron wheelbed and wheel. The latter demonstrate how wheelwrights used to fit iron tyres to wooden wheels. No green space in the Forest would be complete without trees, and examples here are a silver birch, a yew, and an uncommon Champion oak (Quercus rubra) planted by the local council in 2000. In nice weather this is a lovely place for a picnic. If the weather is poor you can sit in the Red Lion and admire Perkins' Piece from the window.

F13 *HMS Hood* and Church of St John the Baptist in Boldre

GR SZ 323993

The Church of St John the Baptist is a squat little church dating from the 11th century. As is often the case there have been many additions and changes over the years. Though a nice church, it would not really stand out if it were not for its charming graveyard and links to *HMS Hood*.

The link with *HMS Hood* is Vice Admiral L E Holland, CB, and his wife Phyllis. *The Mighty Hunt* was Vice Admiral Holland's flagship, and went into action against the German battleship *Bismarck* on 24 May 1942. Within 10 minutes of engaging the *Bismarck* a massive magazine explosion sunk *HMS Hood*. The intensity of the explosion, the swiftness with which the *Hood* sank, and the ongoing naval battle meant that out of 1,418 officers and men only three survived. Vice Admiral Holland went down with his ship.

Mrs Holland and her late husband had been regular worshippers at St John the Baptist so it was a fitting place for a memorial. The centrepiece is a book of remembrance; there is an impressive painting of *HMS Hood*, and other mementoes and information on the locating of the wreck in 2001.

Further links to the Second World War can be found at the back of the church, where Canadian and US flags are displayed. The US flag is a memorial to Americans trained in the New Forest who died on special operations. The Canadian flag commemorates the fifteen Canadian airmen killed while based at RAF Beaulieu and buried alongside British comrades in the graveyard. This graveyard itself is a wonderful place for reflection, with trees and benches as well as headstones to remember the dead.

F14 The blankest spot on the map?

GR SZ 345992

The question mark is actually inappropriate here as there are a number of areas on the New Forest map with less going on. However this is likely to be one of the largest blank areas of open access land. Cartographers, feel free to search out any blank spots larger than 200m^2.

On the map this area, just south of Upper Crockford Bottom, is a featureless plain. The eastern and southern boundaries are paths beside the 30m contour line. In the south-east corner are two tumuli, one encroaching on the plain. To the north a path peters out as it joins the area. The west has a similar-sized area of rough grass mixed with scrub.

In real life the area matches expectations. It is very flat – even the tumuli are flat and hard to spot. The gorse and heather that characterise the surrounding scrubland have almost given up trying to grow here. There are small patches of both but most of the area is simply grass. In the springtime daisies are the highlight of this otherwise blank spot. This is the kind of place that people either find peaceful and calming or immensely dull. If you're bored then quickly head to the fenced-in spring at GR SZ 338989 and splash in the water, bounce on the blanket bog and search for frogs.

F15 Alphabetti spaghetti and vanishing streams

GR SZ 358991

The area around Shipton Holmes certainly raises a few questions when viewed on a map.

Firstly there is the question of the disappearing streams. The eastern fork of Crockford Stream, as it flows from Peaked Bottom, disappears twice. The central fork, north of Lower Crockford Bottom, disappears just the once. To find an answer, best employ wellingtons. In both cases the results will partly depend on how much it has been raining, as the eastern fork is often flowing freely. In dry weather the small stream seems to disappear into the gravelly soil, reappearing as it swells from throughflow around it. The Peaked Bottom channel disappears into something far wetter as the stream simply becomes a bog below Peaked Hill.

The second of the Shipton Holmes puzzles is the strange-shaped boundaries that take up most of square 3599. By my reckoning there are two L shapes, one I, one U or C, one square O, one C or G and one E, W or M. At GR SZ 362993 there is also a '!' On the ground these boundaries are not walls (not enough rock), not fences (no one builds L-shaped fences), but earth embankments. If it has been raining it is easier to spot the embankments due to the long straight puddles they cause. Given the waterlogged nature of the area, they may have been created to channel water away. Another idea is that these are the New Forest's equivalent of the Egyptian or Mayan pyramids. What words could aliens or astronauts make from O, L, L, I, U/C, C/G and E/W/M? The words I've discovered are related to biology and botany and just add to the mystery. Should the Q and U east of Broom Hill be included? The mystery deepens.

F16 Beaulieu rails development

GR SU 374004, 368976

'Beaulieu rails' refers to the ditch and bank that marked the edge of the medieval Beaulieu Estate, and they stretch from East Boldre to East End. In the 18th and 19th centuries the Beaulieu Estate employed hundreds of people in shipbuilding, brick making and agriculture. There were not enough homes for everyone and the Estate resisted building more than a minimal number (such as at Buckler's Hard (G18)).

A squatter settlement began to spring up on Bagshot Moor, along the Beaulieu rails. Bagshot Moor was Crown land, but of poor quality. Initially, due to the risk of eviction, the housing was of poor quality too, but eventually the settlement became accepted and was legitimised. Access to water was a key factor in the community's viability and wells sprang up alongside the houses. Five of these wells are marked on the OS map.

The houses that line Main Road today are a long way from anything you would associate with the modern concept of a squatter settlement. Indeed, there are many examples of typical New Forest cottages. The 18th century dwellings tend to be constructed from timber, cob (essentially soil and a fibrous organic material) and thatch for the roof. Those from the 19th century are usually brick-built and roofed with either local clay tiles or slate. A walk along the edge of the moor or road allows you to inspect the houses and try to work out their vintage.

F17 Lodge Lane

GR SZ 400977

On a wet and windswept winter's day you could be forgiven for thinking this area quite unremarkable, unpleasant even. However, on a sun-drenched July afternoon it is better. Flat fields stretch out in all directions with not a public footpath in sight. Bramble and hawthorn hedges try to shield the fields from prying eyes. Tantalisingly, woodland can be glimpsed – but not visited.

Strawberry farms thrive in the northern part of this square and a punnet of local strawberries certainly enhances a visit. To the south is the interestingly-named Bergerie Farm. This most likely derives from the area's monastic past, as the French word 'bergerie' means sheepfold.

The secret this area is hiding is its wartime past. From 1943 to 1945 two runways crossed squares F17–18 and E17–18 at an Advanced Landing Ground called RAF Needs Ore Point. Needs Ore is thought to be a corruption of Needshore, which fits with the 'ampshire tradition of dropping aitches.

A small track now crosses St Leonards Road at the point where a taxiway and hard standing were sited. Great Bukersleys Copse housed aircraft parking bays for some of the 100 Typhoon fighter-bombers stationed here. Following D-Day the aircraft moved to bases in Normandy and the temporary blister hangars and runways were removed. What is left, other than the flat open land, is a small memorial and a plaque bearing a poem written by local resident Michael Renyard. It reads:

> ***Forest Fields***
> Pause when you see these fields of green
> where once a thousand men were seen.
> Some flying off to war
> to see these fields of green no more.
> Some to stay, to pave the way
> for you to stand on these fields of green.
> Remember them as you stand so free
> gazing o'er the grass and to the sea,
> where once a thousand men were seen.
> They gave for us these fields of green.

F18 St Leonard's Grange Barn

GR SZ 406981

St Leonard's Barn, or St Leonard's Grange Barn, is quite an eye-opener. Located in a quiet corner of the New Forest, on a minor road between two very small villages, it is probably one of the most surprising buildings in the Forest. It is reckoned that when it was first built in the 14th century it was the largest barn in the country. To any passing peasant it must have been the most amazing sight.

The lucky peasant would have witnessed a more impressive building than we do today as the barn was then complete. At some time in the 16th century most of the southern wall was removed and a new barn built inside. This barn remains today, complete with a roof, within the shell of the original.

The gable ends are mostly intact and they are more than 25 metres high, 33 metres wide and around a metre thick. The numerous putlog holes in the gables have been taken over by roosting birds. The north wall is 70 metres long and still intact, supporting the 'new' barn.

The word grange historically meant 'an outlying farm with tithe barns belonging to a monastery or feudal lord'. St Leonard's Grange was one of several attached to Beaulieu Abbey. The size of this barn is an indication of the wealth of the abbey. Its destruction is likely to have been a result of the abbey's dissolution in April 1538.

F19 A view of Gull Island and Needs Ore Point

GR SZ 432986

The area in squares E18, E19 and F19 has changed significantly in the past 100 years though it has had little effect on anyone. Coastal erosion from the Pitts Deep and Thorns Beach areas to the west has resulted in a large build-up of shingle around the mouth of the River Beaulieu. Maps from the turn of the 20th century show marsh and sediment where Gull Island and the Bird Sanctuary to the west are shown today. Needs Ore Point used to be a spit but has now been bypassed and a new coastline developed. In 1986 the gap between the mainland and Gull Island (the Bull Run) was blocked with an extension of the shingle beach, to protect Inchmery Marshes, north of Gull Island.

The reason it does not affect many people is that there is very little public access. Sailors get to enjoy an additional nautical mile of the Beaulieu River but the low-lying marshland is very unsuitable for general recreation. The main beneficiaries are seabirds, of all types. If you are not an expert sea-bird spotter a good book or app is recommended.

For general twitchers and yacht spotters the recommendation is to get down to the shore where Inchmery Lane meets the sea. This allows you a view across to the Bird Sanctuary and birds and yachts will pass you by in their own good time. Very keen twitchers can contact the Beaulieu Estate for a permit to visit the sanctuary.

F20 The Beaulieu River Millennium Beacon

GR SZ 448986

Looking every bit like an eighteenth-century lighthouse and built some distance from the mouth of the Beaulieu River, the name initially does not seem apt. The truth is that boats have had issues with navigation in this area since Nelson's time.

The same longshore drift that formed Hurst and Calshot spits has also affected the course of the Beaulieu River. Rather than flowing south into the Solent, the water at the mouth of the river actually flows north east. Around three kilometres of mud flats, sand banks and gravel deposits including Needs Ore Point and Gull Island block the entrance, frustrating sailors and delighting sea birds.

In good weather most competent sailors could guide themselves between the red and green piles marking the channel. At night, finding the channel is a lot more complicated, so the beacon was built. A beacon is different from a lighthouse as it guides rather than warns. If approached correctly a white light will be clear. Red and green lights will show if you tack too far to starboard or port, allowing you to correct your course.

As the plan to construct a beacon coincided with the approach of the year 2000 it was decided to make it a Millennium Project. The perfect site was found, but it was in the back garden of Lepe House. Thankfully Lord Montagu, owner of the Beaulieu Estate and river, has lots of friends and influence. The owner of Lepe House was amenable to hosting an attractive eight-metre-high 'lighthouse' – and should never have to pay for a drink in the Master Builders or the Montagu Arms again. To see Lord Montagu's influence, glance up at the weather vane.

Officially opened on 8 July 2000, the Beaulieu River Millennium Beacon already looks like part of the New Forest's rich history.

F21 The Watch House

GR SZ 450985

It is extraordinary that we are able to see The Watch House, jutting out as it does into the Solent: many lesser buildings would have collapsed into the water by now. In 2028 the building will have stood guard over the entrance to the Beaulieu River for 200 years. The cottages behind The Watch House were built at the same time to house the newly-formed coastguard, established to combat the amount of smuggling which took place in the area.

The Watch House was originally a boathouse with a bay window for keeping watch over this part of the Solent. It is now a private house, and the bay window is the focal point of the sitting room. Few people will have better views of the Solent and the to-ing and fro-ing along the Beaulieu River.

Although the Solent tends not to suffer from the storms experienced by more exposed parts of the coastline, the window shutters on The Watch House suggest that it can be quite exciting. Old maps indicate that the mouth of the Dark Water moved west from Storie Point before the current buildings at Lepe existed. Large storms do still sometimes close the coastal road here.

Though built to watch from, The Watch House now finds itself watched – it is the focus of many a camera. Great shots include sunsets and catching yachts sailing past. Good luck.

F22 D-Day at Lepe

GR SZ 466989

A small stretch of coastline here in Stanswood Bay was crucial to the success of D-Day. Only around 6,000 men left from Lepe on 6 June 1944 but many of them operated key equipment, such as the 'swimming' tanks which delivered the first heavy weapons to the beachheads. Landing craft at Lepe were able to load tanks due to 'embarkation hards' – special beach-hardening mats, still evident here today.

To the north of the site you can still see the construction platforms for the Mulberry Harbour caissons. These 'bolt-together' harbours were towed across the Channel and assembled in Normandy. They were crucial to the rapid resupply of vehicles, food, ammunition and troops. The caissons were constructed six at a time and then launched into the sea on slipways that are still visible. The rolling-track walls and winch points are also easy to spot.

Following on from men, weaponry, vehicles and harbours, and equally vital, was fuel. From September 1944 the ingenious and well-named PLUTO – the PipeLine Under The Ocean – took fuel from Fawley across to the Isle of Wight and then all the way to Cherbourg. Parts of the pipeline and pumping system still exist on the Isle of Wight but there is no obvious sign at Lepe. The 'dolphins' (four-legged platforms in the sea) were part of a pierhead used by the ships that laid the pipeline.

Some of the most interesting things here are the result of 75 years of sea and weather erosion. The fragments of beach-hardening mats resemble giant broken chocolate blocks and the smooth wood and rusted metal of the winch-gear bases have merged to form beautiful shapes.

G4 Lugden Pond

GR SU 189007

Lugden Pond is unnamed on the OS map but is situated around 100 metres south of the barrow of the same name.

The pond is small but has a lot to recommend it. It's on the edge of mixed woodland with a lot of oak trees close by. A number of trees have succumbed to the pond's charms and are currently rotting in shallow water. In the autumn these logs attract a lot of fungi and if you are lucky you will see small islands of wood covered in mushrooms. During damp periods, the grass beside the pond is flooded. Despite its small size there are some reed beds along the pond's northern shore.

The shape of the pond is a little unusual. New Forest ponds tend to be round, reflecting the gently rolling landscape; Lugden Pond is triangular and slightly resembles a womb. The southerly 'Fallopian tube' travels from the boundary with the Avon Tyrrell estate. The easterly one is much less significant and is not marked on the map; the same goes for the exit from the pond – the water is simply absorbed by Lugden Bottom. A drainage stream of sorts reappears half a kilometre away as Bisterne Common drains westwards.

Though it is not a flashy pond, it is nonetheless a welcome sight for thirsty animals and weary walkers alike.

G5 All Saints Church, Thorney Hill

GR SZ 197997

All Saints Church has a very different feel to many Forest churches. It is believed to be the only church designed by architect Detmar Blow and was consecrated in 1906. It is unusual due to its baroque design, though this is a reflection of when it was built, many years after most Forest churches. It was built on land owned by the Manners family, owners of nearby Avon Tyrrell, for the use of local people including Forest Gypsies who lived in the area. Another unusual feature is that the church faces north–south rather than east–west.

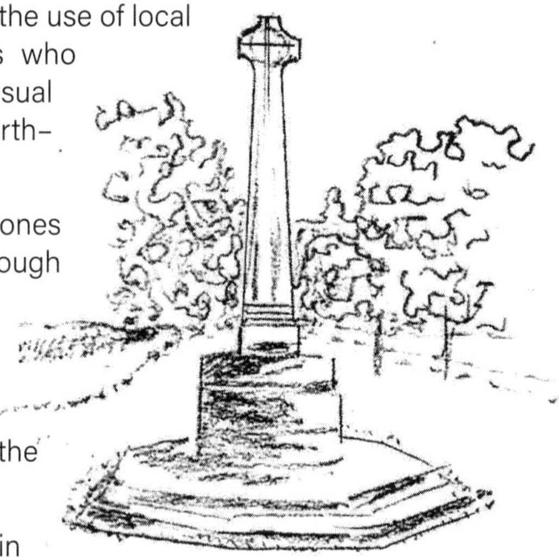

Nestling amongst the headstones in the churchyard is a well, though no longer in use. A number of the headstones are quite exuberantly adorned with flowers, some covered with small cages to prevent animals eating the flowers – plastic or real!

One of the first things you notice in the churchyard is the war memorial. Beside this is a well-kept stone path with sheltering arcade of trees. There are lots of young trees in the churchyard with benches dotted around allowing you to admire the area, including the valley behind the church. In fact it's a good venue for plane spotters as Bournemouth (Hurn) Airport is nearby.

If the church is open the interior is well worth a look. Inside is a remarkable mural by Phoebe Traquair, with themes spanning war, the New Forest and religion. In a style later copied by the Beatles in the design of the album cover for *Sgt. Pepper's Lonely Hearts Club Band*, famous faces are included in the mural. People to try and spot include Louis Pasteur, Lord Tennyson and William Blake; many of the other characters are members of the extended Manners family.

G6 The New Forest Hats

GR SZ 214997

Hats are very common in the New Forest but might not be quite what you expect. King's Hat, 3km south east of Lyndhurst, is one of the best known, but there are at least ten others including another King's Hat. In this area there are three hats quite close together, the best of which is Great Hat. Bell's Hat and Cardinal Hat to the south and north respectively are also worth a visit if you have time.

In the New Forest the word 'hat' has traditionally been used instead of 'clump.' Clumps do exist (such as Avon Clump in square G4 and Robin Hood's Clump in M3) but tend to be less common. All three hats in this area have grown larger in the generations since they were named and are now small woods.

It is believed that the term 'hat' derives from the resemblance of a group of trees on top of an incline to a form of headgear. If you think of the type of hat worn by the Puritans who sailed on the *Mayflower* you would be on the right track.

G7 Holmsley Train Station

GR SU 231007

Both sides of the slip road from the A35 bear all the signs of a train station bar the rails and trains. The first clue, though, is the name of the road from Burley: Station Road.

On the west side of the road is a cycle path and the significant remains of what was clearly a long platform. Just west of the platform is a bridge which used take the railway over a stream. The stream here is quite substantial, bearing in mind its source is only 250 metres away. A bog adds to the water flow and this is kept at bay with a significant retaining wall. On top of the wall is a nice curly wrought-iron railing , curled even more now thanks to the intervention of a tree. At some stage a rudimentary building – use unknown – has been fashioned out of sleepers. Lots of other clues exist including parts of rail sticking out of the ground, brickwork and fence posts.

On the opposite side of the road is the former Holmsley railway station. Now a tea room, Holmsley station had famous visitors such as General Eisenhower, Kaiser Wilhelm, and Queen Victoria's son, Prince Edward pass through its waiting room. There's a train station theme and feel to the tea room which is well worth a visit after exploring the area.

G8 Wilverley Inclosure

GR SU 250007

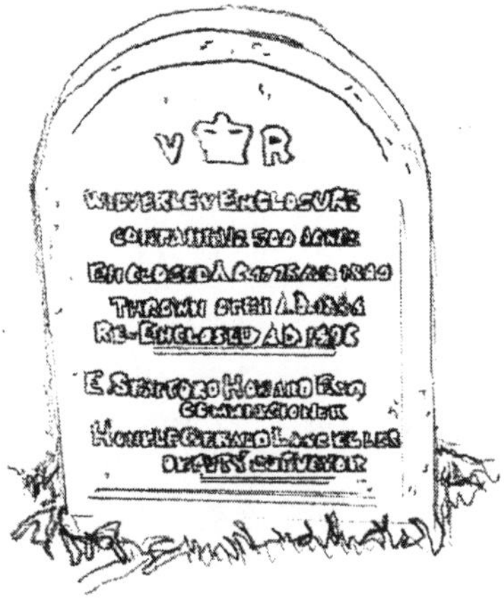

'VR
Wilverley Enclosure
Containing 500 acres
Enclosed AD1775 and 1809
Thrown open AD 1846
Re-enclosed AD 1896
E. Stafford Howard Esq
Commissioner
Honble Gerald Lascelles
Deputy Surveyor'

This sign spells out Wilverley's past. It was enclosed to grow timber to keep the Admiralty happy. One reason for the re-enclosure would be the proximity of 'Castleman's snake' (or 'corkscrew') – the railway which ran alongside the southern edge of the modern-day inclosure.

Wilverley Inclosure is now a hive of activity. There are a dozen car parks within a mile and people have a choice of the wooded inclosure or the plain. Dog walking, jogging and cycling are all very popular with the inclines proving a tough test of joggers and cyclists alike.

There is a mix of dull plantations and beautiful, almost alpine, scenery. The path junction at GR SU 244009 provides stunning trees and vista. Here you can see the divide between ancient conifers on one side and broadleaved trees on the other. Both are impressive and benches strategically placed along the main paths to allow you to admire the view.

Wilverley is a place for exploring and getting away from the main tracks; you are likely to be rewarded with lots of wildlife including roe deer. That said, if you sit by the inclosure sign for 30 minutes and watch the world go by, you will also have an enjoyable time.

G9 Victorian Railway Bridges

GR SU 258000, 266002

On an 800-metre stretch of dismantled railway line are three bridges dating from the mid-1840s. All three are in very good condition and play a role in supporting Route 2 on the National Cycle Network. When complete, this cycle route will extend from Dover to St Austell and currently measures 361 miles (581 km). If you are planning a shorter journey this stretch of cycle path links Brockenhurst with both Burley and Christchurch.

Starting in the west, the first bridge is a stunning brick-built example that allows walkers and ponies to stroll under the cycle path. The flanks curve round in a really pleasing way showing why Victorian architecture is still held in such high esteem today. As well as the path there is a little drainage in damp weather from Yewtree Bottom. Open railings allow a view from the cycleway into the surrounding moorland.

Bridge two is a mixture of bricks and stonework with a high brick parapet. This bridge allows a minor private road to cross perpendicular to the cycle path at the start of a long cutting.

The final bridge is possibly the most impressive. An angle of 40° to the road above means the brick work is all slanted and a testament to the skill of the workers who created it. This bridge also has pedestrian/pony tunnels either side of the main arch.

Whether you visit one bridge or three, enjoy the architecture. If you are cycling to Cornwall or Kent - bon voyage!

G10 First day on the job in Hincheslea Bog?

GR SU 277005

If you do not get too close, Hincheslea Bog is a lovely place to visit. This particular spot allows you to view the bog from the safety of a good track. At this point the stream shown on the map at Long Slade Bottom has lost its momentum: the contour lines have flattened out and a long, wide bog has formed. There is a small, square brick-built island a short leap from the track which the adventurous may wish to visit.

The island is not shown on the OS map, but as it is only 1m^2 this is not surprising. A slightly larger, four-sided object is shown, beside the railway at GR SU 277004. In real life, unlike the tiny island, this does not exist. This anomaly might suggest a map error, possibly by a novice cartographer. There is further evidence of beginner's errors on the map, which you can contemplate as you walk around the area.

The bridge and path junction at GR SU 278004 is a little confusing. The map correctly shows the cycle path on top of the former railway embankment but suggests a bridge then crosses above it from the track. The bridges in square G9 show how they should be organised should you be interested.

At GR SU 280007 a stream flows beside a path for a short distance before turning east and heading under the path: *towards* a spring, defying all logic!? Trying to find the spring that the stream flows into is not recommended as it is very boggy here and it would in any case offend your common sense. In fact it is so boggy here that on the map Hincheslea Bog is completely surrounded by OS marsh symbols. For some reason, though, this 'Hincheslea Bog' is marked in black whereas the 'Hincheslea Bog' a kilometre to the south west is blue.

There is a lot of cartographical geekery involved in this square, so feel free just to walk around and enjoy the views.

G11 Clapham Junction, New Forest style

GR SU 293004

Clapham Junction is the busiest train station in Europe in terms of trains passing through, with 17 platforms and rail lines heading off in several directions. One place you can travel to from Clapham Junction is Brockenhurst, the New Forest's major train station with four platforms. An impressive station in its own right, Brockenhurst boasts a modern pedestrian bridge linking all the platforms as well as an old-fashioned level crossing to catch out motorists. An odd feature is the pedestrian bridge that carries a right of way over the tracks and station. This bridge has no steps down to the station and essentially ignores the station's existence.

The highlight of this square is not Brockenhurst station but Lymington Junction, 1½ km to the south. Lymington Junction is not a stop but is the New Forest's only railway junction. For aficionados of railway bridges this is a must-see. Though none of the bridges is particularly impressive, what they lack in grandiose architectural chutzpah they make up in numbers.

Until May 1964, barely a year after the infamous Beeching Report, there were three lines leading from Lymington Junction. A southerly branch follows Three Beech Bottom and takes trains to Lymington Pier and the Isle of Wight ferry. The south-westerly main line links London Waterloo to Weymouth. The defunct westerly route used to link Southampton to Ringwood and then Poole. Part of this line is now used as a cycle path and provides a pleasant route to the village of Burley.

A 2-km drive from the B3055 bridge over the main line south of Brockenhurst will take you over and under five bridges by the time you re-cross the Lymington branch line just north of Milking Pound Bottom. Walking or cycling introduces you to another three bridges over or under the first kilometre of main line south of the junction. Bridge fans – fill your boots.

G12 The path to Roydon Manor

GR SU 317003

If you are lucky enough to visit Roydon Woods Nature Reserve during March or April (or possibly a bit later) you will witness an amazing profusion of wild flowers of all types, but mainly yellow varieties.

In the open fields in front of the impressive manor house daffodils prevail, though these are escaped domestic flowers rather than their wild cousins.

On damper ground there are primroses. Primroses appear to have found their Utopia here as they line most of the tracks and spread into the nearby fields. April 19th is Primrose Day. Prime Minister Benjamin Disraeli (1804–1881) loved these little flowers, and Primrose Day marks the anniversary of his death – an appropriate day to visit.

Also in the mix are dandelions, whose leaves are suitable for salads if you catch them early, and celandines. Both of these flowers are nyctinastic, which means they react to night-time by 'sleeping' – something to watch out for if you're here early or late.

Last, but by no means least, are marsh marigolds (or kingcups). These are usually found near the bridge over the Lymington River as they enjoy very damp ground. The flowers are supposed to resemble a cup fit for a king but using one to drink from the Lymington River is not recommended.

Whilst in the area it is worth listening out for green woodpeckers. If you are lucky enough to spot one you will see that they also have a yellowish hue, in keeping with their springtime surroundings.

G13 Haywards Farm's 'mushrooms'

GR SZ 327994

Haywards Farm has a wonderful display of staddle stones on either side of Thistle Lane. Staddle stones are the mushroom-like stones often used to support important agricultural buildings. The word staddle comes from the Old English 'stathol', which means foundation. They have been a common sight in the English countryside for over 300 years.

The stones are almost always in two parts, with a conical base topped by a much larger capstone. This design prevents vermin, such as rats, being able to climb the legs of the building. For this reason most food stores, such as game larders and granaries, were elevated upon staddle stones. A second benefit is that raising the building off the ground allowed air to circulate, keeping crops dry.

The stones on the west side of the lane at Haywards Farm are now decorative, but also serve to stop people parking on the grass. On the east side of the lane is a traditional barn on staddle stones, a sight which is becoming less common as wooden buildings decay, leaving only their attractive supports. These are then snapped up by people wishing to ornament their gardens with something old and rural. Enjoy these great examples.

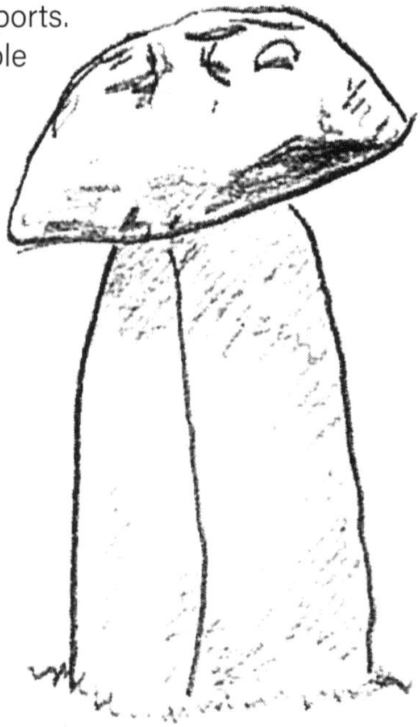

G14 Two Bridges Bottom

GR SZ 343997

The first thing to mention about Two Bridges Bottom is that it has no bridges. This, and the boggy nature of Upper Crockford Bottom, means that wellington boots are a good idea. Where the bridges were and where they went is a mystery. This is not an upland area, where flash flooding could have carried them away, but it is pervasively damp so maybe the bridges simply rotted. At the time of writing some kind soul had laid a scaffolding plank across the stream on the path connecting the trig point to the car park.

The feeling you initially get in this square is emptiness. There are no roads or houses, no structural boundaries and of course no bridges. Further investigation will soon uncover the remains of the airfield in the north east of the square and tumuli in the north west. If you close your eyes and open your ears you will quickly pick up bird song.

The damp southern part of the square, around 'No Bridges Bottom', is a popular breeding area for several rare species of birds, including the nightjar, curlew, Dartford warbler and woodlark. The birds are very fast and shy so spotting them takes time. During nesting time in the spring you are advised to stick to the paths and keep dogs on leads or do not bring them. If you can find a dry spot to sit this is a lovely area to enjoy nature.

G15 RAF Beaulieu

GR SU 358006

The OS map gives some hint as to the past uses of Beaulieu Heath. The obvious features are a large flat area with an unfenced track extending across almost 2km^2. Satellite images add the elongated A-shape inside the track and show two concrete areas in the east and north west.

In the early 1940s RAF Beaulieu would have been an impressive sight. It was used by British, Czech, Canadian and American pilots from 1942 until it was returned to the Forestry Commission in 1959. All manner of aircraft were based here, from British Typhoon fighters to American Marauder bombers, taking part in the Battle of the Atlantic and supporting the D-Day landings. Airmen and crew stationed at Beaulieu had the use of a gym and cinema, and lived and worked in the numerous buildings and hangars that once stood here.

Present-day Beaulieu Heath is very different. The decommissioned airfield has a car park with an information board, and a 200-metre-long stretch of the former runway for people to fly their model aircraft. From here, pilots once took off on their immensely dangerous missions, and for some, RAF Beaulieu would be the last place they set foot on British soil. It's a very poignant spot and a walk or cycle around the former taxiways is highly recommended.

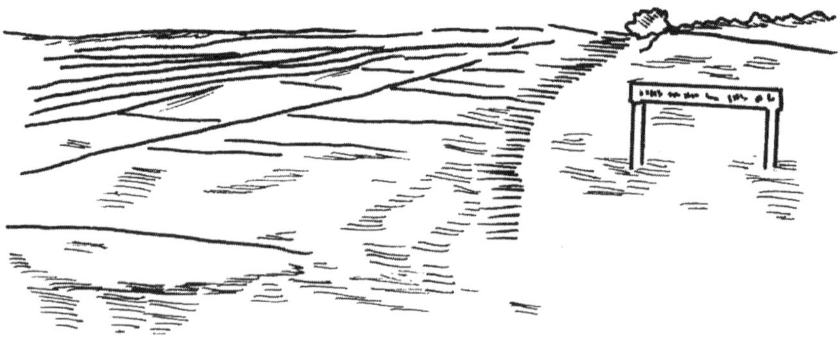

G16 Beaulieu Cemetery's unusual grave

GR SU 382007

Beaulieu Cemetery is unusual for a number of reasons. Firstly, it's not in Beaulieu, but 1.5km away to the north and still within the parish. Apart from Grindingstone Cottages opposite the site, it is completely surrounded by farmland.

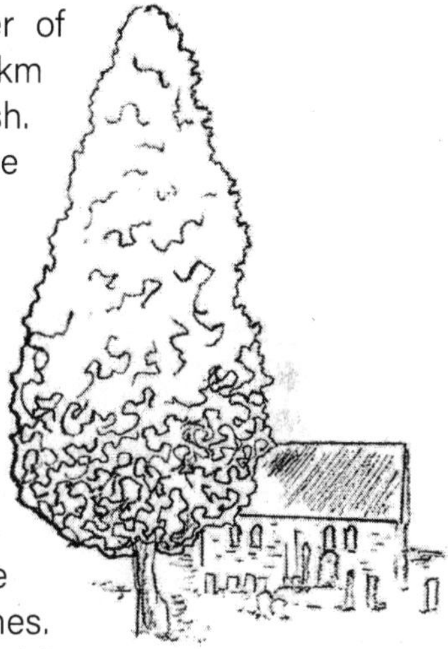

The focal point of the Cemetery is a massive fir tree which puts other trees to shame. There is also a chapel, a very simple building with stained glass windows but usually locked. It fits in snugly with the gravestones and allows the trees to dominate the scene.

Although there is no Commonwealth War Grave sign there are a number of military gravestones. One is unusual because it is for a female soldier. Corporal Cecilia Phillips was in the Auxiliary Territorial Service (ATS) and passed away on 4th July 1946 aged just 26. There were just 300 women killed while serving with the ATS, a voluntary service for women formed in 1938 and disbanded in 1949. Other notable members of the ATS include 2nd Lieutenant Elizabeth Windsor and Winston Churchill's daughter Junior Commander (Capt.) Mary Spencer-Churchill.

Cecilia Phillips died in Thanet, but is probably buried here because her parents lived in Beaulieu.

'DUTY CALLED BUT LOVE REMAINS. GONE BUT NOT FORGOTTEN'

G17 The path from Beaulieu to Buckler's Hard

GR SU 401010

Though only brushing the edge of this particular square the walk from Beaulieu to Buckler's Hard is a treat.

The journey includes grasslands, ancient semi-natural woodland, evergreen plantation and amazing riverside walks. There are also great views of the stunningly expensive-looking houses overlooking the river and an insight into the area's architectural history. At one point the sandy bank is almost four metres high and you're overlooking the houses on the far bank.

Much of the area you walk through is now being managed to provide high-quality natural habitats for wildlife. The variety of grassland, woodland and wetland mean it is ideal for nature lovers as the flora and fauna are constantly changing. Change is a feature here: in the past the woodland and riverside would have been busy in a completely different way.

During the 16th and 17th centuries this area was an industrial centre. The woodland would have been full of woodcutters felling timber for the boatyards at Bailey's and Buckler's Hards. The boatyards employed hundreds building ships for the Royal Navy. From 1790, a kiln fired millions of bricks using clay dug from nearby pits. Many of the buildings on the Beaulieu Estate, as well as the imposing Royal South Hants Hospital in Southampton, were constructed from these bricks. Clay was transported to the kiln via a narrow-gauge railway through the forest and bricks were transported on barges down the Beaulieu River.

Information boards give much more detail about the flora, fauna and history as you pass through this amazing place.

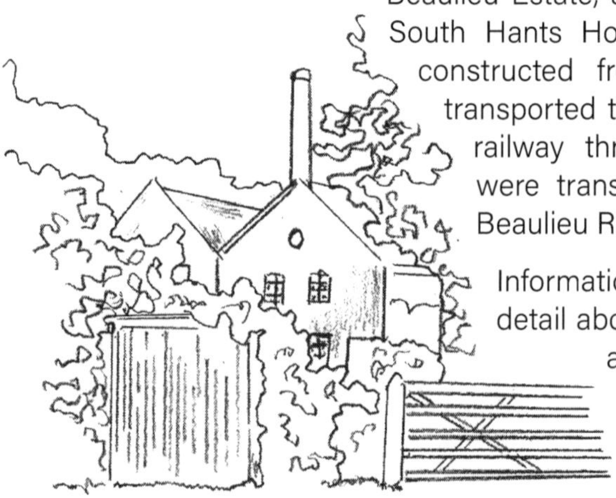

G18 Buckler's Hard

GR SU 409001

Of all the hamlets in the New Forest, Buckler's Hard is probably the most impressive. The main street is gravel with terraces of houses on either side. The houses to the west are three storeys high and those to the east only two. Upon leaving any of the buildings by the front door no walls or fences spoil the view, just manicured grass. At the end of the main street is a stunning view of the Beaulieu River.

Entry to most of the public buildings and the main car park involves paying for admission. You are free to visit the area via the Master Builder's pub (car park to the rear) or by foot along the Solent Way. Visiting the Maritime Museum is highly recommended: it tells the story of the area's nautical past.

If you had visited Buckler's Hard in 1781 the scene would have been very different. The Master Builder's pub was the home of Henry Adams, builder of *HMS Agamemnon*, Lord Nelson's first command. The ship was built using wood from the nearby forest and launched from the hard into the Beaulieu River. Hundreds of craftsmen and women helped launch more than 50 Royal Naval vessels from this tiny village. A school, now a chapel, operated on the main street and is another attraction that can be visited.

If you had visited Buckler's Hard in early June 1944 you'd have found that the boat-building industry had returned. Torpedo boats were built throughout the Second World War and the Beaulieu River was chock-full of boats of all kinds ready to embark on D-Day. It's remarkable to think that this tiny place played an important role in both the Battle of Trafalgar and Operation Overlord.

G19 Exbury Bridge

GR SU 422004

Exbury Bridge is a wonderful representation of British idiosyncrasy. It is called Exbury Bridge by Ordnance Survey because it is set in the middle of the Exbury Estate. The Exbury Estate calls it Gilbury Bridge, because it allows access to Gilbury Hard. Exbury itself is named after the Exe, the former name of the River Beaulieu. This word is a corruption of the ancient British word 'Iska', meaning fishes. If you look into a clear part of the River Beaulieu you will see it was aptly named, with large sea bass a common sight. Beaulieu, from the French for 'beautiful place', is perhaps equally apt.

The role of the bridge is to allow visitors to Exbury Gardens (the public part of the estate) to cross the lane which bisects the Rothschild-owned estate. That land owned by one of the richest men in the country can be cut in half by a public road leading to a small public footpath and hard is a delight. Gilbury Hard is not particularly impressive but the views of the River Beaulieu are.

Exbury Bridge itself is probably unique in the New Forest. A 4m-high single span stretches across the quiet lane. The underside reveals its brickwork to common folk, whilst the Rothschilds and paying customers are treated to plastered balustrades above. Whether you travel under or over the bridge depends on your budget and your interests – enthusiasts of small steam trains will want to visit the gardens!

G20 Stepping-stone bridge

GR SU 445005

Stepping-stone bridges are very common in some parts of the country – especially Dartmoor, where they cross wide rivers and are labelled on the map. However, they depend on large erosion-resistant rocks such as granite being locally available. The New Forest has no such rocks so stepping stones are very rare. In fact, this may be the only example.

Depending on recent rainfall this may or may not be a good spot to visit. The whole woodland smells richly luxuriant in the wet and the boggy areas beside the path come alive and feed Dark Water. As a result, during wet weather, Dark Water runs fast, deep and murky. It also runs over the stepping stones on this rather unique 'bridge'. Most of the characteristics of a bridge are there – steps, a handrail all the way across and a footpath sign – but there is no deck to walk on.

The four stepping stones are great if the tops are dry, but they can be under quite a few centimetres of water (ten centimetres in not uncommon). The 'stones' are man-made, though this is preferable to local sandstone, mudstone or even chalk from mid-Hampshire.

If the stepping stones do not take your fancy just ten metres downstream a strapping tree trunk lies across the stream. In the wet it's pretty slippery though . . .

G21 Dark Water

GR SZ 450998

A very aptly named place: the waters of Dark Water are indeed dark. They act as a sort of black mirror, reflecting a shadowy image of what lies above. The footpath that accesses the northern part of Dark Water is more of a causeway, keeping most of the water off the path.

In true New Forest style, an area of little perceived value to farmers has become an area rich with nature. The boggy ground and water host a wonderful selection of plants, bushes and trees. Around the dark water are the resplendent greens of oak, birch and other trees. Every kind of moisture-loving plant is represented. Sometimes these plants produce the most amazing flowers, so be prepared for flashes of white, yellow and pink amongst the deep camouflage of the greens, browns and blacks. On damp days, especially, your nose will be assaulted by the smells of the vegetation.

The whole of Dark Water is under threat. The future of the road between Lepe and Exbury is at risk from constant high-tide flood damage. If the county council decide to abandon the road, the tidal sluice gate will go with it, allowing the sea to inundate this low-lying area. So perhaps a dark future for Dark Water?

G22 Luttrell's Tower

GR SU 477009

Built in 1780 for MP Temple Simon Luttrell, Luttrell's Tower boasts a stunning view of the Solent. The property, which has been owned for over 50 years by the Landmark Trust, is let out as a holiday home. But is it an amusing folly or a lookout tower for a corrupt parliamentarian?

Mystery surrounds the exact reason for its existence but rumours of a history of smuggling are supported by a number of the building's features. Most significantly, the tower gives a superior view up and down the Solent, allowing for the monitoring of incoming goods and, perhaps more importantly, incoming customs officials. A tunnel from the beach to the cellar would make movement of contraband quick and easy. The beach here is relatively shallow and the waves generally small, simplifying loading and unloading. Whatever the truth, Luttrell's Tower, sometimes called Eaglehurst Tower after the more recent house built at its base, is a wonderful folly.

Not to be outdone, the natural environment is also wonderful. Hillhead is an apt name for the area as the cliffs on this stretch of coast are over ten metres high – the highest in the New Forest. Their survival, given that they are composed of gravel and sand, is surprising; but these cliffs are protected by the broad beach and by mature holm oaks, whose roots bind the soil and whose evergreen foliage acts as a year-round windbreak.

H1 Wattons Ford

GR SU 137017

Any ford that has a sign stating 'Deep Water' beside it raises a few questions. Most of the questions connected to Wattons Ford are easily answered. The obvious question is: 'Can I ford the river here?' and the short answer is a clear 'No'.

Wattons Ford lies just outside the westernmost limit of the New Forest. The park boundary here resembles a fist making a leftwards grab for the River Avon and missing it by a hundred metres. A right of way leads from a kink in the Avon Valley Path (also avoiding the river). The right of way is signposted but entry is discouraged, and not just by the 'Deep Water' sign. The gate is awkward, the path overgrown with small trees as well as nettles and grass, and the ground is muddy. The path ends up at a mass of reeds with no way through. There is nothing that resembles a ford. On the way back the river can be glimpsed, glinting as it flows south.

From the western bank you'd have to be a big fan of stinging nettles to even get near to the river. A Hampshire County Council sign, ignoring the fact that it is in Dorset, announces: 'Deep water'. Another sign is hidden among reeds and nettles. Eventually, as the wind blows the foliage aside, it can be seen to read: 'Bisterne Estate. Private Water. Not Navigable . . . Canoes . . .' (unclear but obviously negative). Again the reality of the ford is absent.

The wonderful website www.wetroads.co.uk/hampshire.htm proves that crossing the ford is possible, though very impractical. It was last attempted by vehicle in 2004 and by horse and cart in around 1900. Our rights of way are very important and this one would have been very useful in conditions of low water before the A31 was built. Any attempt at crossing by foot would almost certainly involve being rescued from the mud or swept down to Christchurch Harbour, though there are worse places to visit.

H2 The legend of the Bisterne Dragon

GR SU 148012

The legend of the Bisterne Dragon involves a number of New Forest sites. Most of the Bisterne Estate is inaccessible but the eastern side of the church grounds gives views across the area. The fields of Lower Bisterne Farm can also be viewed from the Avon Valley Path and were perhaps the site of numerous misdeeds by a cruel dragon.

The historical archive at Berkeley Castle, Gloucestershire, tells the tale:

> *'Sir Moris Barkley the sonne of Sir John Barkley, of Beverston, beinge a man of great strength and courage, in his tyme there was bread in Hampshire neere Bistherne a devouring Dragon, who doing much mischief upon men and cattell and could not be destroyed but spoiled many in attempting it, making his den neere unto a Beacon. This Sir Moris Barkley armed himself and encountered with it and at length overcam and killed it but died himself soone after. This is the common saying even to this day in those parts of Hampshire, and the better to approve the same his children and posterity even to this present do beare for their creast a Dragon standing before a burning beacon. Wch seemeth the rather more credible because Sir Morice Barkley did beare the Miter with this authentick seale of his armes as is heare underneath one of his owen deedes exprest bearing date ye 10 of Henry 6. An Dni 1431.'*
>
> (https://bisterne.com/legends-and-stories/)

Modern variants of the story suggest that a green dragon lived on Burley Beacon (Castle Hill) and came to Bisterne to eat. Local people were being impoverished by the increasingly greedy dragon so Sir Moris Berkeley and two ferocious hounds came to kill it. A monumental battle followed and both dogs were killed. Sir Moris, with a suit of armour covered in bird lime studded with glass, carried on the fight and eventually slew the dragon in a field in Lower Bisterne Farm. Overcome by the trauma of the battle and the loss of his hounds Sir Moris then lay down to die at Bolton's Bench in Lyndhurst.

If you do not believe in dragons, simply substitute dragon for 'ferocious wild boar' and you might find the story more believable.

H3 Broad Ford

GR SU 170017

The New Forest has many fords but there are unlikely to be any others as wide as this one.

The key reason for this is that the unnamed stream (known downstream as Sopley Brook) runs along the track that is trying to ford it for ten metres, before turning south and continuing to the Avon at Sopley. Whether this was part of the plan is unclear, as it is both unconventional and inefficient. However it is strangely pleasing to contemplate the slightly iron-brown water flowing across an assortment of concrete slabs, mud, sand and stones.

If they are to keep their feet dry here, pedestrians need both the boardwalk and the bridge. This is a place where Adventure Poohsticks can be played as there are many obstacles for any stick to navigate. Due to the length of the Adventure Poohsticks' course it is important that the sticks can be easily identified (a forked stick, or one with an acorn attached for example). The umpire may also need wellington boots to monitor contestants' behaviour.

It is not clear if this is the crossing that nearby Sandford is named after as there are also fords to the north and west. However, this track is part of the old route from Burley to the Wattons Ford crossing of the River Avon.

H4 Boundary stones on Kingston Great Common

GR SU 187022, 186025, 186026

This area of bog forms the border between the parishes of Ringwood and Burley. It's a very arbitrary straight line, similar to one you would find in the Sahara. The reason for the lack of detail in the boundary would become evident if you were to foolishly attempt walking in a line from Lugden Barrow to Knave's Ash Barrow. This area contains some of the deepest and remotest mires in the New Forest, and walking north of the boundary stone at GR 186026 is considered dangerous.

The stream that forms in Cranes Moor and drains south remains nameless until it reaches Sopley, where locals call it Sopley Brook. The cartographer who failed to name the stream has also missed a boundary stone between its neighbours. There is also a bonus concrete post for those who like to visit everything in an area. The stones have a simple BS inscribed in them and are all quite easy to spot, though your feet might be damp by the time you find them.

Further boundary stones are visible on Lugden and Knave's Ash Barrows. The one at Lugden is overgrown but can be found amongst the gorse bushes. The barrows predate the current boundary and have simply been used as convenient and obvious places to set stones.

Any journey around this area will involve seeing lots of wildlife. Deer are common; the area is part of Kingston Great Common National Nature Reserve and is a staging post for many birds, including swallows migrating south.

H5 Slap Bottom

GR SU 205019

If Benny Hill, the Southampton-born comedian, ever visited the New Forest, I would imagine this would have been his destination. Benny Hill was the king of slapstick comedy during the 1960s and 70s with gags such as 'Just because nobody complains doesn't mean all parachutes are perfect'. Any slapped bottoms in his shows would quickly result in a slapped face.

The best bit about Slap Bottom is its name, the origin of which is unknown but could come from 'slope'. The area itself is dissected by a slow-moving drainage stream which gets wider the further upstream you go. At Slap Bottom it becomes a bog. To the south of the stream is an area of damp grass, then heather and gorse. North of the stream is an area of mixed woodland, mainly birch beside the stream and conifers further away. Slap itself is a hillock covered with birch and holly and would be entitled to the name Slap Hat (see square G6).

Although Slap Bottom itself may not be as picturesque as some parts of the New Forest a walk along the bottoms is very worthwhile. There are a number of paths north of Holmsley Bog which take you across valleys as far as Scrape Bottom should you wish to risk it. The best of the bottoms is certainly Shappen Bottom, where, if the ponies are frisky, you could hear the hoofbeats pound as they race across the ground.

H6 Greenberry Bridge

GR SU 218015

There is no longer a bridge here, nor a need for one. There are also no berries of any colour. There is a right of way, though it has fallen into desuetude. When the Southampton to Dorchester railway was built many tracks were provided with bridges or tunnels. As these crossed private land rather than Crown land they were made rights of way. Now the railway has gone the area has full public access but the rights of way remain.

What exists on this spot today is the confluence of a very good cycle path from Burley to Brockenhurst and a track from the centre of Burley to Holmsley and beyond. The bridge has long since collapsed and the brickwork that remains is in poor condition. Gorse and ferns, somehow thriving in the stony soil, are attempting to engulf what is left.

400 metres to the east of Greenberry Bridge is the site of a former railway gatehouse. It is now a very modern and stylish home. In marked contrast to this is square G9 where you can still see railway bridges in all their Victorian glory.

H7 The Goats' Pen

GR SU 224018

Plainly, the historical Enclosure* on Goatspen Plain is a shadow of its former self. The enclosure that you see today would not stop an elderly guinea pig from escaping. A lot of imagination is needed to imagine a pen full of noisy bleating goats, tended by a goatherd. It is more likely the 'Goatspen' is a corruption of someone's name – perhaps the owner of the pen.

However, whilst you are using your imagination, consider a fabulist called Aesop visiting this enclosure in the distant past and perhaps witnessing the following scene:

> *'A goatherd was one day gathering his flock to return to the fold, when one of his goats strayed and refused to join the rest. He tried for a long time to get her to return by calling and whistling to her, but the goat took no notice of him at all; so at last he threw a stone at her and broke one of her horns. In dismay, he begged her not to tell his master: but she replied, "You silly fellow, my horn would cry aloud even if I held my tongue."'*

As Aesop suggested, there is no point trying to hide what cannot be hidden. The truth that cannot be hidden here is that the goats' pen is a bit of a disappointment, as it is 1% reality and 99% imagination. But now that your mind is active try to work out how nearby Scrape Bottom got its name. And once you've done that, consider Anthony's Bee Bottom.

*Note on usage. The old spelling 'Inclosure' is used commonly in the New Forest to cover the enclosure of common land by the Inclosure Acts. The goat's pen is an enclosure in the sense of a coop or fold.

H8 Not a lot to log, but there is the Duckhole Bog

GR SU 249022

There are many things shown on the OS map in this square, but they don't all quite tally with reality. The Naked Man is labelled '(site of)' so not even the most optimistic visitor would expect to see a naked man there*. What you do find there is a tree with a fence around it, marking the spot where rumour has it that highwaymen and smugglers were hung. There are many yarns about the origin of the name but the naked man and the original tree are long gone.

At Wilverley Post there is nothing to speak of other than nondescript fence posts, certainly not warranting a mention on the map. Spy Holms, to the north, has no spy**. Even the small pond shown on the map in the inclosure next to Wilverley Post is not in evidence on the ground.

Something that does exist is Duckhole Bog. The New Forest has a lot of bogs; they vary hugely and often seem to have their own personality. First impressions of Duckhole Bog are of its situation, tucked away within a moderately steep-sided valley. Most of the valley slope is bog and water drains unhurriedly into the main channel. Peat-stained water then flows slowly through the valley.

Pools resembling infinity bogs sit beside the path for frogs or ducks to enjoy. The water is oily-looking and often filled with algae but supports an abundance of wildlife. Reeds, heather and birch all mix it up with water lilies which flower in June.

There are often ducks, but if not other birds will generally step in to entertain you.

*Note that it cannot be guaranteed there will not be a naked man here as people are weird and wonderful.

**As above, but for spies.

H9 The bogs

GR SU 268022

This square has some interesting names as well as the most named bogs in one square mile. Horseshoe Earth sounds Tolkien-esque whereas Bats Bush might be a place to find a bat, or perhaps a Robin.

The main features here are the bogs. Holm Hill and Red Hill both have their adjacent bogs which help form the Silver Stream leading past Crab Tree Bog. Hincheslea Moor is worth a visit whatever the weather. On a bleak, wet day the sense of isolation is out of all proportion to the short distance you need to travel from a car park to get there. On a sunny day the vista is immense. There are a few trees for shade if needed but this is an area of heather, gorse, fern and grass. Up and down the small hills and valleys you can see the colours of the main vegetation change depending how much water is in the soil beneath. The season is important as well, as heather can be brown or purple; gorse dark green or yellow; and ferns light green or brown.

The paths across the area are accessible, even with a buggy, and the boggy bits can easily be avoided or experienced depending on your wishes. In fact, the pathways across the bogs are probably the highlight of a walk here, especially by the Silver Stream. In spring you can see tadpoles, fish and dragonflies, an amazing array of bog plants and a profusion of insects.

H10 The centre of the New Forest

GR SU 288015

If you draw a line in the New Forest from the northernmost point to the southernmost, and another from the easternmost to the westernmost, you arrive very close to this spot, near Brockenhurst. You would actually be in a private field, and very probably annoying a local farmer, so for simplicity the nearest publicly accessible point has been chosen.

Counting the mile squares would be another method of ascertaining 'the centre' and would take you to the middle of Lyndhurst. So both villages can claim to be to be the most important in the New Forest!

Channels drain this area, with the North and South Weirs draining into The Weir. 'Weir' may refer to an old name for the area or may simply be a slight corruption of general usage: in this case, 'a small dam used to divert water'.

During dry periods the weirs appear to have succeeded, with the area next to the small pond ideal for a picnic in the geographic heart of the New Forest. When the weather is wet, the flatness of the ill-named Furzy Hill means surface water sticks around and wellingtons are recommended. In the North Weirs the ground is damp all year round.

H11 Brockenhurst High Street ford

GR SU 297022

Brockenhurst's main shopping street is not called 'High Street' as it is in many larger New Forest District towns and villages such as Totton, Lyndhurst and Hythe. However, none of these places have a ford (of the water variety) traversing their main thoroughfares. The main street in this picturesque village, the largest in the National Park, is called Brookley Road. According to the dictionary a brook is a small stream. This brook is indeed small, so small that it only occasionally rises high enough to trickle across the road, moistening the tyres of cars travelling to the newsagent's or grocer's, and living up to its nickname: the splash.

The brook has its source in boggy ground to the west of Brockenhurst. The southerly branch rises in Hincheslea Bog before joining The Weir, its northerly and much straightened neighbour. After the ford the brook provides an excuse for a footpath for a short distance before joining the much more impressive Ober Water, later to become the Lymington River.

H12 The oldest (yew) tree in the New Forest

GR SU 305017

There are a number of contenders for the title of 'Oldest tree in the New Forest', including this one. Most sources suggest it is either this tree, in the churchyard of St Nicholas' Church, Brockenhurst, or the Knightwood Oak, south west of Lyndhurst (K9).

This tree is very likely indeed to be the oldest yew tree in the New Forest, with an age of around 1,000 years. That sounds impressive until you learn that yew trees have to be 800 years old to be regarded as ancient. The oldest known yew tree in the UK, at 2–3,000 years old, is the Fortingall Yew in Perthshire. What is for sure is that St Nicholas' yew tree is large. It takes around 12½ seconds to pace around it, which is a lot longer than Usain Bolt takes to run 100 metres.

The tree also upstages the church which does not seem to want to compete. Having appeared in the Domesday Book, St Nicholas' Church is the oldest church in the New Forest and of a similar age to the yew tree next to it.

The church and cemetery tell the story of Brockenhurst as a hospital village during the First World War. A hospital for Indian and then Kiwi casualties was set up here due to the good transport links with Southampton, where most hospital ships berthed. Around 23,000 casualties were treated in Brockenhurst, and over 100 Indian and New Zealand troops and three Belgian civilians are buried in the Commonwealth War Graves cemetery in the churchyard. The churchyard is beautiful and a fitting testament to those who gave their lives for others.

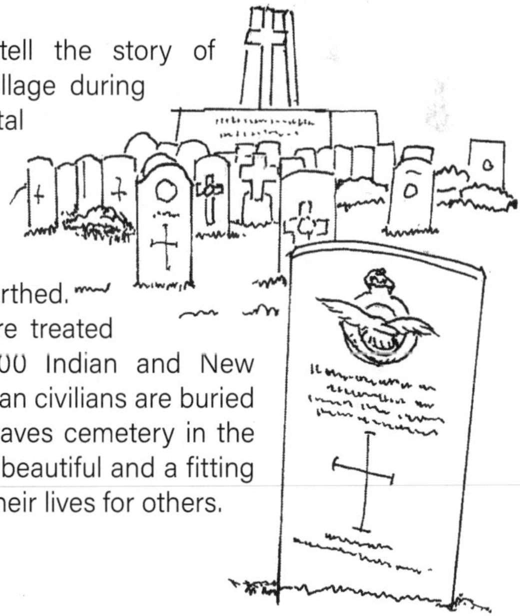

H13 Hidden remains of the Second World War on Furze Hill

GR SU 329016

The area around Furze Hill and Lodge Heath formed part of RAF Beaulieu's dispersed sites. This walk of around 500m starts at the footbridge (GR SU 328018) and finishes at the start of the bridleway at Dilton (GR SU 332015).

Beside the stream and up the hill there is a succession of clues that this used to be a habitation. In the stream there are bricks and a few metres from the footbridge a ceramic drainage pipe continues its work. Wartime plans indicate that there was a sewage disposal site here. Presumably the stream here was used to transport sewage into the Lymington River and then across the Channel to occupied France.

Hidden amongst the trees are areas of concrete, brickwork and tiles. In a few cases fallen trees reveal foundations they covered seventy years before. There were many buildings here including mess facilities and toilet blocks used by both American and British aviators and support staff.

At the top of the hill are concrete roads, in most cases still in good condition. Just inside Dilton Farm boundary, but perfectly visible from the public right of way, the pièce de résistance – two Handcraft huts. The huts, which are very similar to Nissen huts, are slightly dilapidated but are an indication of what many of the airfield buildings looked like. Several further examples lie out of public sight two hundred metres to the east.

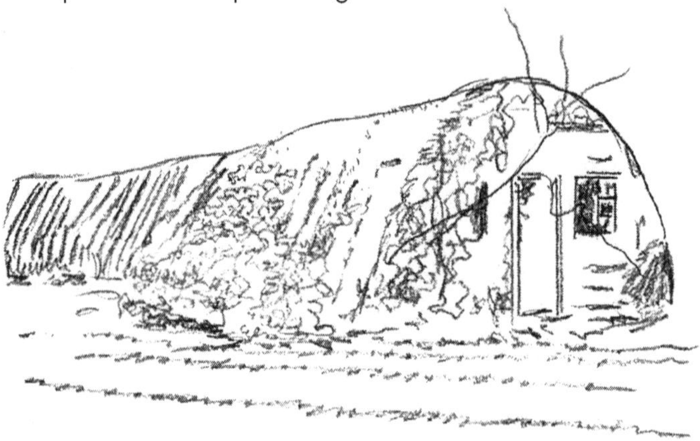

H14 Lodge Heath tank

GR SU 337018

Any grid square that shows a tank and a Pudding Barrow within a hundred metres of each other is worth an investigation.

'Panzer, Sherman or Churchill?' war buffs will ask. Water, actually. Nonetheless this very impressive water tank has military origins. Lodge Heath was built up extensively in the early 1940s with infrastructure to support the nearby airfield on Beaulieu Heath (G15). The foundations of many buildings are dotted around and the camp's roads now form the grid of a campsite. The water tower, still in military green, sits amongst a number of shielding trees. Despite its great height and size it is remarkably well camouflaged.

Pudding Barrow is a Neolithic round barrow. If you are imaginative you might think it resembles a blancmange or a filled doughnut. Excavations have established that any treasure hidden in the barrow was removed many centuries ago; the modern fence around the site is more to prevent modern day trespassers, like mountain bikers and barbecuers. Many similar barrows could once be found across Beaulieu Heath but they were bulldozed to make way for runways during the Second World War.

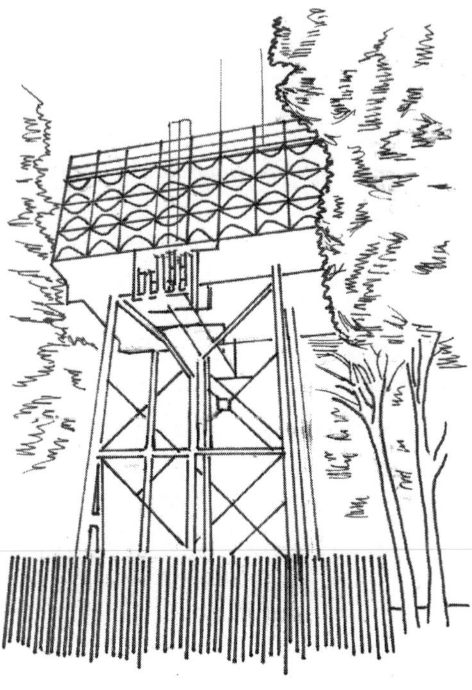

H15 The Hatchet Pond challenge

GR SU 365012

Hatchet Pond is the largest pond on Crown Land in the New Forest. It was formed by damming a small stream to power the mill in square H16. It is a beautiful place to visit, with a huge amount of wildlife living in and around it. Together with other ponds in the area, it forms the basis of the Hatchet Pond challenge.

The aim of the challenge is to score 100 points by visiting a number of the 10 ponds in square H15. Different ponds are worth different numbers of points, depending on the ease of access.

- Hatchet Pond GR 368014 – 5 points
- Round pond in road triangle GR368013 – 15 points
- Tiny pond south of B3054 GR 367012 – 10 points
- Square pond north of car park GR 366012 – 5 points
- U-shaped pond south of car park GR 365011 – 5 points
- Tiny pond to the west of Hatchet Pond GR 360012 – 30 points
- Pond opposite small wood on B3055 GR 353017 – 15 points
- Square pond just east of the previous pond GR 355017 – 15 points
- Pond on boundary of Hawkhill Inclosure GR 356018 – 20 points
- Pond just south of Furzey Lodge GR 368021 – 20 points

Bonus points:

- 1 point for any kind of gull on the pond
- 2 points for a duck on the pond
- 3 points for a swan on the pond
- 4 points for a goose on the pond
- 5 points for a sea eagle or kingfisher near the pond!
- (-1 point if the bird flies away because of you)

H16 Hatchet Pond and Mill

GR SU 369015

Hatchet Pond is a large pond, but despite its size its catchment area is very small. The stream feeding into the southern part of the pond is only about the same length as the pond; likewise the northern feeder stream.

The pond was created in the early 18th century to power a mill. The embankment built to contain the pond is an impressive structure in itself. To the east of the pond is the former mill, now an attractive three-storey house. The rear garden can be viewed from the road and boasts a number of special features. A large earth embankment is the first, now topped by a road and with a brick retaining wall on the wet, west side. The large pipe jutting out of the embankment, just above the top of the ground floor, looks rather like Saddam Hussein's 'supergun' and is probably a 'unique selling point' in estate-agent-speak. At ground level there is a metal structure that looks like it covers an opening – probably where a water wheel stood.

On the pond side of the embankment you can just about make out where the pipe intake would have been. Water now drains from the north-easterly corner of the pond. A drain and overflow pipe travel under the road and a straight drainage channel, unnamed, can be seen heading through the Beaulieu Estate, finally reaching the the Beaulieu River at the site of the Royal Southampton Yacht Club.

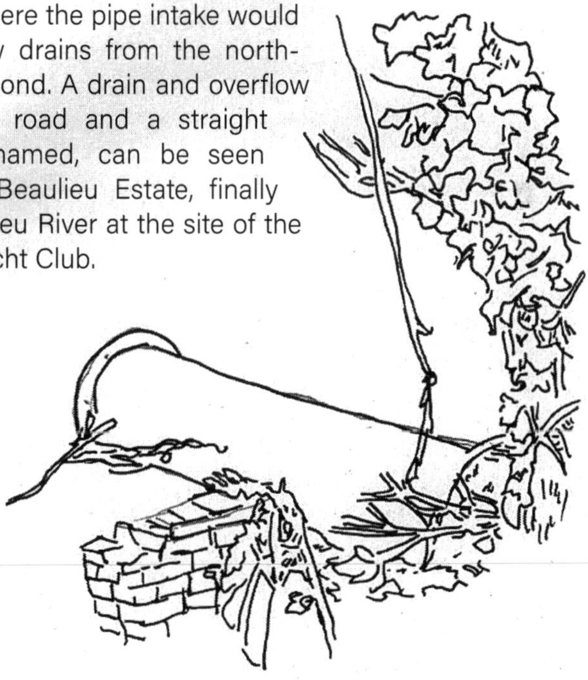

H17 The bus shelters of Beaulieu

GR SU 392025, 388024, 386022

Beaulieu is a hugely interesting village in many ways. One attribute that is often overlooked is its eclectic mix of bus shelters. It may seem a strange thing to fixate on, but Beaulieu could have the best selection of bus shelters in the known world. It would also be a great surprise if anywhere in the unknown world has better bus shelters as well.

Beaulieu is a small village and the route served by the bus stops gets only one bus a day. When you have nearly 24 hours to wait for your next bus a nice shelter is small consolation: but better than nothing.

The first shelter does not act as a bus stop any more but provides people with a comfortable place to pause when posting a letter in the nearby post box. A solid four-person concrete and wood bench is open to the elements on three sides and bears a more than passing resemblance to a cricket pavilion. Best avoided on wet and blustery days, it's an ideal place to watch the traffic go by on sunnier days. Perhaps you'll even catch sight of the daily bus.

The second bus stop is the most grandiose and the best to shelter in from poor weather or a zombie apocalypse. Solid brickwork, possibly removed from the remains of the neighbouring Cistercian abbey, make for an imposing but compact building. Three arrow slit windows provide defence from attack from the east and west. However, from the south you have to rely on a kissing gate to keep donkeys and zombies out. Although the top of the shelter appears to have a parapet it would make a poor battlement as the lack of crenellations would expose archers on the roof. None of this detracts from its role as a perfectly good bus shelter, but if you gaze across the mill pond you'll see that one house has a cannon in the garden, seemingly aimed at Lord Montagu's manor house.

Lastly we have a bus shelter that at first glance seems the most traditional. It's a solid wooden structure with a bus stop sign on one side and a bin on the other. Inside is a bench which further investigation reveals to be double-sided. To the south is a view of the road but the northern view is of the mill pond. A sign reveals this to be a great spot for birdwatchers.

As well as bus shelters Beaulieu has a world-famous motor museum, a manor, abbey remains and a wonderful selection of shops and eateries.

H18 The great gates

GR SU 417014

The great gate of Summer Lane shuts off entry to Steerleys Copse. What is in Steerleys Copse, other than trees, is a mystery, as there are no rights of way passing through this corner of Beaulieu Parish.

The gate is not great compared to a gate of a palace or manor house. However, it is impressive compared to any of the other gates enclosing woodland in the New Forest. Standing 2.4m tall and slightly over 3m wide, the two gates are significant constructions. Made of iron rather than wood, they need cross bracing in both directions to support themselves. Posts are the key to any successful gate and these posts are fittingly substantial. Slightly taller than the gates, octagonal, and cast iron, surely these gateposts have to hide something more interesting than a small copse?

Indeed these forbidding gates, guarding a dark copse on Summer Lane, do have a history of keeping secrets. During the Second World War the whole of the Beaulieu Estuary was occupied by the Admiralty. All the hards were used for building or repairing smaller vessels, such as torpedo boats. Before D-Day Mulberry Harbours, along with countless additional shipping involved in the invasion, were assembled on Beaulieu River. Perhaps the most famous secret hidden behind the great gates could be the time spent there by the future author, Lieutenant Commander Nevil Shute Norway. During the war Nevil Shute was based in Exbury House, known as *HMS Mastodon*, and he based his book *Requiem for a Wren* on his experiences. Another of his projects here involved building secret rocket-propelled aircraft for the impressively-named Directorate of Miscellaneous Weapons Development. Secrets aplenty.

H19 Rolleston Golf Course

GR SU 433025, 441025

The story of Rolleston Golf Course was related to me by the husband of a former workmate when we met by chance in King's Copse Enclosure. Though parts of this historic golf course are in imaginary squares H20 and I20, the names Green Lane and Roughdown suggest it extended to H19 as well.

The story went as follows:

> *Just after the First World War the Rothschild family of Exbury House (G19) built a golf course in this area and called it Rolleston Golf Course. During the week local villagers were allowed to use it for free. At weekends the Rothchilds entertained guests there so locals had to steer clear.*
>
> *When the Second World War came the land was turned over to agricultural use, in common with parks and gardens across the country. The golf course never recovered from this, and the former pavilion became the village junior school. The school building still has a weather vane with a golfer as decoration. The rest of the course became school fields or agricultural land.*
>
> *Two of his colleagues had relations who knew the golf course. One was a caddy and the other used to sneak on to 'scrump' golf balls lost by the rich and famous.*

The OS map from 1945 clearly shows a golf course between what is now marked as Roughdown and Sports Ground. Google Maps shows that a part of the course was retained in the Sports Ground. The old pavilion has been sold off and is now part of a new development next to a newly rebuilt school called Pavilion Gardens (sadly without a golfer-adorned weather vane).

H21 Air raid shelter

GR SU 457011

At first, the reason for an air raid shelter on this sliver of open-access land between a series of fields is puzzling. The shelter is of a fairly standard design with thick brick walls, including a blast wall covering the doorway, and a concrete roof. Though not designed to withstand a direct hit, these shelters would stop any shrapnel such as stones or bits of tree from hitting people. These days the strength of the shelter is being tested by a tree resting a branch on the roof.

To work out why such a fine air raid shelter was built in the middle of nowhere you need to draw a line between Stansore Point at Lepe and Fawley Oil Refinery. This reveals that the shelter is almost directly on the route of the PipeLine Under The Ocean (PLUTO) during the Second World War (see square F22).

This pipeline, and the numerous buildings connected to it, would have been a prime target for bombing raids. Mopley Pond had a pumping station close by and there were holding tanks on Badmiston Common. The consequences of a hit on or near the pipeline would have been pretty catastrophic so an air raid shelter was pretty essential for the people working here.

Undamaged by Luftwaffe bombs in a twentieth-century battle, it remains to be seen if the tree or shelter will win the battle in this century.

H22 Blade Runner versus the swing bridge

GR SU 477023

Fawley Power Station most definitely is not in the New Forest National Park. It is surrounded by the park, and was due to be included but managed to swerve inclusion, so it is not subject to the stringent planning rules that apply to national parks – something its owners would want to avoid.

Fawley's design is very much a product of its proximity to the New Forest. When it was built one of the design briefs was that it must be a suitably cool design for the entrance to Southampton Water with its New Forest backdrop. Extensive use of glass, topped off with a rotunda-style control room, gave the power station a futuristic look. So cool was the design that it featured in several films, including *Rollerball*, *Mission: Impossible – Rogue Nation* and *Solo: A Star Wars Story*.

Since decommissioning, the Fawley site has been used to store and finish wind turbine blades. At 82m long these cannot be brought to Fawley by road, so they are transported on *Blade Runner II* – a suitably sci-fi name for a boat visiting a sci-fi site. The boat must contend with a swing bridge in order to drop off its cargo. To circumnavigate the site you must also contend with the swing bridge so try not to arrive at the same time as the boat. If you have to wait awhile you could visit the short 'jetty to nowhere' which starts and finishes on land. There are also the architectural delights of the current and future environment to enjoy. One suggestion involves building a revolving restaurant at the top of the power station chimney, though this may prove to be pie in the sky.

*Note: it is looking increasingly likely that this site will be extensively built upon. Hopefully you will still be able to identify some of the features described here!

H23 Calshot Spit

GR SU 488025

Calshot Spit has something for everyone.

Possibly the biggest draw are the views of the Solent and Southampton Water. Due to the shape of the shipping channels, larger ships have to take a wide arc on their way into the busy port of Southampton. Oil and gas tankers berth on both sides of Southampton Water, at Fawley and Hamble refineries. Car transporters export British-built Land Rovers, Jaguars, Nissans and JCBs, returning with all manner of European and Japanese vehicles. Ferry spotters will enjoy watching the fast and slow ferries crossing back and forth what is often called 'the most expensive stretch of water in Europe'. In 2008 Prince William caused ructions when he flew an RAF Chinook helicopter to his cousin's stag do on the Isle of Wight. Press indignation was inflamed by the fact that he first flew from Hampshire to Woolwich to pick up his brother Prince Harry! Was it cheaper than the expensive ferry? Cruise ships are the jewel in Southampton's crown and watching from Calshot Spit as a 10-storey-high cruise ship rumbles past is an incredible sight.

If staring out to sea has inspired you there are many opportunities to get on or in the water at Calshot. A shallow beach on the eastern side of the spit provides decent swimming opportunities when the weather is nice. This is also the side where experienced windsurfers and sailboarders demonstrate their skills. On the more sheltered leeside of the spit kayaking and dinghy sailing are popular as well as bird watching in the nature reserve.

If the weather is inclement, the old flying boat hangar houses a café, a ski slope, the largest climbing wall in Hampshire and the second shortest velodrome in the world (the shortest track in London, Canada, is four metres shorter at 138 metres). You can also read about the history of Calshot as an RAF base, an airport and the scene of the Supermarine S6's Schneider Trophy win in 1929. Another wet weather option is the small but interesting castle that (sea level rise permitting) will celebrate its 500th birthday in 2039.

13 The Castleman Corkscrew

GR SU 166040, 168036

In 1847 the Southampton to Dorchester Railway Company opened a line that linked a number of Dorset towns to the port of Southampton and the London main line. The principal protagonist for this railway line was a Wimborne solicitor named Charles Castleman, and when the line was opened its meandering style gave rise to its nickname, 'Castleman's Corkscrew'.

This section was closed in 1964 but there are still clues to its existence. The most obvious is at the southern end of the bridleway where a short length of track crosses the road. Beside the track is signaller's cottage No. 14, and in 2019 the former signalman's wife was still living there. Across the road and stream is a small hut that was connected with the railway but is on private land and has fallen into disrepair.

At the next road junction is signaller's cottage No. 15, extended a great deal since the railway closed. Most of the old level-crossing gateposts are still in place and can be seen in their heyday in a photo on a rickety information board just north of the cottage.

Continuing north will take you into Ringwood where you can pick up the southbound Avon Valley Path. The two paths can be linked by road and east-west paths in two places: south of the sewage works to Upper Kingston, and Moorhouse Farm to either North Kingston or Sandford.

14 Kingston Great Common National Nature Reserve

GR SU 185033

According to Natural England, as of 19 March 2020 there were only 224 National Nature Reserves, covering just 363 square miles, in England. Kingston Great Common is one of these reserves, on account of its flora and fauna. The area is a mix of pine woodland, heathland and mire.

During dry periods most of the area along its boundary on the OS map is accessible. When wet, wellingtons are a good idea and straying too far south or east is not recommended.

As a National Nature Reserve it is also the kind of area where dogs are best kept on a lead. Conservationist, dog lover and New Forest resident Chris Packham has courted controversy in the past by suggesting the public be banned from some areas. His prime concern is to protect ground-nesting birds but he may have mellowed, as this quote from August 2018 shows:

> *'I have a passion for conservation, the New Forest is an area which draws dog owners, and dogs have an impact. I am very keen to educate dog owners to change . . . their behaviour so we're all more compatible with the New Forest'*
>
> (www.advertiserandtimes.co.uk/chris-packham).

Birds to be found on the Common include European stonechats, common chaffinches, woodlarks and Dartford warblers. In the mire bog asphodel, bog myrtle, bogbean, marsh St John's wort, marsh arrowgrass and marsh pennywort all live up to their names. Lizards, dragonflies and butterflies are at home here as well as a wide range of mushrooms.

All in all, Kingston Great Common is both a wonderful place to visit and well worth protecting. We can do this by not venturing too far into the mire, by not bringing dogs during nesting season and by picking up any litter we see. Alternatively, there are 221 other places to visit.

15 Burley Castle

GR SU 199039

Castle Hill is the site of an Iron Age fort that could be as much as 2500 years old. Like most other 'castle' sites in the New Forest, it has no castle.

The attraction of the site today is the same as it was all those millennia ago – the view is wonderful, although in the past watching out for hordes invading from Dorset might have been the main concern of those manning the fort. Recommendations these days would include birdwatching in the direction of Strodgemoor Common and exploration of the fort's remaining ramparts.

To the north and west nature provides a 20–30-metre slope steep enough to slow down any Iron Age warrior. The man-made ramparts that complete the defences are for the most part intact. The earth mound is several metres high in places, and evidence remains of the ditch that would have surrounded the rampart.

If you visit in the winter a sweet chestnut tree on the edge of the southern rampart will provide a tasty snack to roast at home. In Dickens' *A Christmas Carol*, chestnuts were given by reformed character Ebenezer Scrooge to the family of his poor clerk Bob Cratchit, and in the final scene Tiny Tim and his family toasted Christmas, 'while the chestnuts on the fire sputtered and cracked noisily'. *Bon appétit*!

I6 Burley

GR SU 211030

Burley is one of the most-visited villages in the New Forest, and rightly so. There are numerous points of interest around the triangular junction that marks the centre of the village. A walking tour, starting at the war memorial and going in whatever direction you wish, is recommended. Here are some of the highlights:

The war memorial is an impressive Portland stone Celtic cross. It was erected by a colonel and his wife grateful that their two sons and a son-in-law had survived the First World War.

The Burley Inn has some notable turnstiles, designed to keep out all but the thirstiest ponies. Beside the inn is the Burley Millennium stone.

The Burley Commemorative Clock celebrates the Queen's Diamond Jubilee in 2012. Look carefully around the border of the clock for representations of village life.

Opposite the entrance to Burley Manor is one of Thomas Eyre's stones, marking the distances to Ringwood, Christchurch and Lymington. Thomas Eyre was the house steward to the Lord of the Manor in the late 18th century and responsible for many local acts of charity.

The Queen's Head pub dates from 1685 and is central to many smuggling stories involving secret tunnels to Burley Manor and cellars of treasure. Opposite the pub is another Thomas Eyre stone, commemorating the restoration of peace (temporarily, during the Napoleonic Wars) in 1802. Just along the road from the stone is the Church of St John the Baptist, dating from 1839, and home to two wooden mice.

After the Witchcraft Act was repealed in 1951 Sybil Leek, a Burley resident, revealed herself to be a white witch. The media storm that followed led to Sybil being dubbed 'Britain's most famous witch' and has left an enduring legacy in Burley in the form of witch shops.

Burley rocks are a rare find but the wall of Dawson Engineering on Pound Lane displays both rocks and classic cars. It is believed that the rocks were transported here from Mill Lawn (I7) where there is an area called Burley Rocks but where no rocks are to be seen.

17 Cotton grass

GR SU 227032

Cotton grass is synonymous with wet ground so boots are recommended for an exploration of this square. On a sunny day the area around Mill Lawn Brook looks to be full of luxuriant grass, as the 'lawn' in the title suggests. Closer inspection reveals that the greenness of the grass is due to an abundance of water. An extensive bog to the north of Shoot Wood drains into channels and eventually the brook. This bog is spongy and vibrant and in early summer is marked by the white seed heads that resemble cotton.

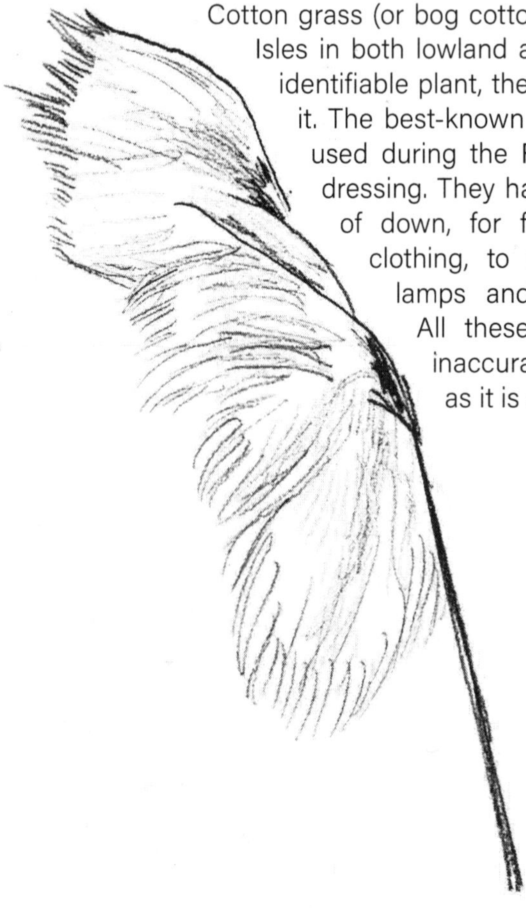

Cotton grass (or bog cotton) is found across the British Isles in both lowland and highland areas. An easily identifiable plant, there are plenty of stories about it. The best-known is that the seed heads were used during the First World War as a wound dressing. They have also been used as a type of down, for filling pillows and insulating clothing, to make wicks for candles or lamps and with tinder to light fires. All these stories are true: the only inaccuracy is the name 'cotton grass' as it is actually a sedge.

18 Tree detective

GR SU 250032

At the path junction to the west of Ferny Knap Inclosure is a small stand of intriguing trees. They appear to form an avenue along a small track. Only half a dozen survive, along with a group of silver birch fenced in around a rectangular pond. This would be the perfect spot for a pony pond, if it wasn't for the fence. Neither the trees, the pond nor the fence are featured on the OS map.

It is best visited on a breezy day, when the wildly fluttering leaves sound like an angry swarm of bees and draw your attention to the trees. The noise is noticeable from quite some distance – a classic sign of the aspen, whose flattened leaf stalks cause the leaves to vibrate. They are often known as quaking aspen for this reason. Another typical feature of aspens is that they occur in small groups, because aspens send out suckers underground that produce a new, genetically identical, tree. However, the leaves of these trees are not the typical aspen dark green on top with a light green underside; the undersides of these leaves look silver. This is most noticeable when they flutter in the wind.

Similar to the aspen but with whiter leaves is the white poplar. Both are in the willow family, but the key recognition point of the white poplar is its leaf colour, which is caused by a white, hairy coating on the underside of the leaf.

The colouring of the leaves and the fluttering suggests that these trees are both aspen and white poplar, which happens to be the answer. The grey poplar is a natural hybrid between the two and shares many of the characteristics of both. There is a lot of variation, so the grey poplar is more of a range than an exact species.

The beauty of these trees, along with their relative rarity in the New Forest, is probably the reason why they have survived in an area with a lot of logging activity. For the most enjoyable sensory experience visit when the wind is 20mph (35kph) or more.

19 Rhinefield House

GR SU 263034

Rhinefield House is one of the most impressive buildings in the New Forest. It is a hotel now so you can visit as a customer and enjoy the maze, carp pond and various artworks in the formal grounds. Some of the views from outside the grounds give you a better perspective, with the south-west corner of the periphery a great vantage point.

The house is a combination of Jacobean, Tudor and Gothic styles and a look inside is recommended if you are in the mood for a spa visit or afternoon tea. Its site, along with £250,000, was given to one Mabel Walker by her father on the occasion of her marriage to Lt. Edward Munro, RN in 1877. This gift was a considerable fortune and no expense was spared in creating a luxurious house and formal gardens. A glorious house needed a glorious title, so the Walker-Munros began to call themselves 'Lord and Lady of the Manor at Rhinefield', which did not impress the actual Lord and Lady of Brockenhurst and Rhinefield.

A possible link with much more exalted personages is the story that in December 1648, on his way from imprisonment on the Isle of Wight to London for his trial and execution, Charles I met Oliver Cromwell in a hunting lodge at Rhinefield. If they did have a meeting here, it obviously didn't go very well.

I10 Ober Shade

GR SU 288039

Confusingly enough, shade is a New Forest term for an open area where cattle gather. You will often find a shade on a hilltop or by a pond or stream where the breeze or water will cool the animals.

In the case of Ober Shade the area is quite flat. Ober Heath is open country, so any breezes from the south west will reach this corner. The attraction to cattle and ponies is the Ober Water stream. This has a large catchment area, extending to an area of bog north of Burley named Harvest Slade Bottom. A slade is a valley but there does not seem to be an example of a named slade beside a shade.

Ober Shade is a popular place for animals to gather. As well as the breeze and an ample supply of water the trees provide the shade that the name seems to hint at. It is also a nice place for people to gather. The stream provides entertainment for adults and children alike and many grassy paths lead across Fletchers Green and beyond. The nearby historical site of Queen Bower Hunting Lodge harks back to a time when animals would have been ill-advised to gather at Ober Shade.

There are many 'shades' in the New Forest but just a few are named on the OS map.

I11 The Water Works

GR SU 291041

Just south of Bolderford Bridge, lying under the 14 spot height on the OS map are two brick structures. The first one, which often sits in a pool of iron-tinged water, contains a metre square of weeds and resembles an over-engineered planter. The Victorian brickwork is in good condition but damaged metalwork indicates another structure previously sat atop the bricks.

Further south, following an occasionally wet channel, is a larger structure. Around twice the size of the first one, this building includes a doorway revealing a large metal bollard. This is a hydraulic ram pump and very similar devices are still in use today. The fact that it has neither rusted away nor been scavenged is remarkable.

Walk down to the river in an easterly direction and you will find the inlet pipe. Given the proximity of New Park estate it is very likely that the pump extracted water from the river to be either stored for collection or pumped directly to the house. New Park, rather like the New Forest, is very old and was a favourite hunting lodge of King Charles II in the seventeenth century. Charles kept his mistress, Eleanor Gwyn, here as well, for days when the weather was inclement.

I12 Balmerlawn and Balmer Lawn

GR SU 304032

Separated from Brockenhurst by the Lymington River is the small ribbon development of Balmerlawn. To the north of Balmerlawn is its namesake and origin, the Balmer Lawn. Lawns are quite common in the New Forest, though they are a little different to the lawn you may have at home. They tend to be large open areas of grass, smaller than a moor, wetter than a plain but much drier than a bottom. Balmer Lawn is a place for Commoners to graze their animals and has been extensively drained, though with limited success. Balmer is believed to be a corruption of Palmer, who presumably had some claim on this area, in the same way Butt did on the lawn on the opposite side of the A337.

In the south-west corner of Balmer Lawn is a hotel named after it which has become a Brockenhurst landmark. The hotel has an interesting history, starting life as a hunting lodge in the 1800s and almost being destroyed by fire in the 1970s. In common with much of Brockenhurst the hotel was taken over by the military during the First World War. The building was large enough to act as the main hospital for wounded New Zealand servicemen arriving at Southampton Docks. Further reference to this can be found in square H12.

During the Second World War it was Canadian forces who took over the hotel. A staff college for the first part of the war, it became the HQ for the Canadian preparation for D-Day. After the war, a maple tree was planted in the hotel grounds to commemorate the sacrifice of Canadian forces.

Now it is a hotel again, you can follow in the footsteps of Winston Churchill and Dwight D. Eisenhower (who visited a great many square miles of the New Forest) by dropping in. If your timing is good you can catch a game of cricket being played beside the hotel at the home of Brockenhurst Cricket Club.

I13 **Railway tunnels**

GR SU 324033

There are many options for crossing over the railway in this square, but only one right of way goes under the railway. It is shown on the OS map as resembling a green boomerang which has got wedged under the railway. There are no obvious paths leading to or from the tunnel but all the open land beside the railway is easily accessible.

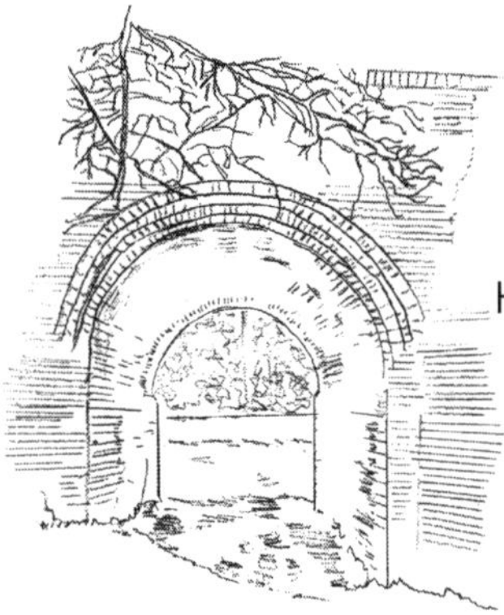

When you visit the pedestrian tunnel you will immediately notice that there is a very similar one less than 50 metres away. This tunnel was built for the intriguingly named Etherise Gutter that rises 2km north of here near the top of King's Hat (hill). Etherise means 'anaesthetize with ether' which doesn't seem to have much relevance to this quiet corner of an inclosure. Gutter is a typical name for a watercourse in the New Forest, with its roots in the Old French words guitere, goutiere, meaning a gutter or spout.

Though the root of the name is unclear, the route you take under the railway might be a dilemma. Should you walk dry-shod through the pedestrian tunnel or add some excitement to your journey by sharing the other tunnel with Etherise Gutter? During dry weather the stream doesn't provide much of a challenge, but when it has been raining wellingtons may need to be mobilised.

An enjoyable 7km round trip involves starting at either of the car parks at Ivy Wood (GR SU 315024) or Balmer Lawn (GR SU 308032) and heading north along the main drainage channel across Balmer Lawn. From here visit the well at GR SU 309050 and then the spring at GR SU 310052. You can then follow Etherise Gutter all the way to the Lymington River before returning to the car park.

I14 A speedway track?

GR SU 338036, 346038

The glories of this square are numerous and all lie beside the railway. Though none of them rival the Arc de Triomphe or Grand Canyon they are curiosities to tickle the fancy of those who are looking to have their fancies tickled. They are listed here from west to east on the north side of the line.

Three culverts cross drainage channels flowing from the south. The first two are shown on the OS map, with one flowing from an interesting pond in Ladycross Inclosure. The concrete culverts are wide enough for a tank to cross. They seem over-engineered for a small footpath but do their intended job of allowing the occasional walker to pass. An attractive pond sits between the first two drainage channels and is worth a look.

The most curious feature occurs just before you reach the rail crossing. There is a large concrete circuit in the shape of the eye of a needle. The curved part of the track is banked in the style of the Indy 500 circuit. At the other end is a similar, but more offset, curve, allowing for a circuit of around 500 metres. The reason for this track is revealed by *NFNPA Archaeology* on their immensely detailed New Forest Knowledge site:

> *'During the 1950's & 60's the Forestry Commission started upgrading the timber extraction tracks in the Forest by making new gravel tracks around the inclosures. They needed to experiment on the mix of sand, gravel and clay so they could find out what was most hard wearing.*
>
> *As such they laid out this concrete circuit which had patches in the central section which could be laid with the experimental mixes. A lorry would then be set to driving over and over the mix again and again with the turning circles at each end to prevent the need for lots of manoeuvring each time they got to the other end.*
>
> *At the Woodfidley one you will note a little to the west is an oblong pond, this is where they dug the clay from for the experiment.'*

Mystery solved.

(https://nfknowledge.org).

115 Rowbarrow

GR SU 357041

The area of woodland around Rowbarrow is probably best explored during the Autumn equinox. The pitter-patter of falling acorns adds a little fun and the oaks and birch trees which predominate are turning from green to amber. If you time your journey well it may feel as if there are a million daddy longlegs accompanying you. As they are a great food source for birds and bats it would also be a good time for some spotting.

Any zigzag route through the woods here is pleasant. Ponies will have created dozens of tracks through the autumnal ferns and squirrels are always busy planning next year's menus. Mushrooms are also abundant in this area, providing another chance to spot common and less common species.

The stream or drainage channel shown on the map here rarely flows. When it does, it doesn't stop at the track, as indicated on the map, but continues north through the Bishop's Dyke to Rowbarrow Pond.

This is an area for meandering and looking up at the giant gnarled oaks and down at the huge branches that have collapsed over the years. If you have more time Honey Hill and Tantany Wood make a worthwhile extension to any visit.

I16 Hartford Bridge

GR SU 380037

The water running under Hartford Bridge is special water. The banks of the river here are also special, as is the river bed. What makes the Beaulieu River special is that it is one of the only privately-owned rivers in the world. As any angler or kayaker can tell you, access to rivers can be difficult at the best of times. In this case, though, the very water flowing in the river channel is owned by Lord Montagu.

Ownership of the Beaulieu estuary and surrounding estate has been in the Montagu family for over 400 years. For 400 years before that, Cistercian monks owned the river and would have been the ones to shake their fists at you as you floated by in a hollowed-out log. Sadly Henry VIII's transfer of ownership did not open up access to the Beaulieu River as, in keeping with many of the estates in the southern New Forest, public access is restricted. The marshy nature of the estuary also restricts access to the waterside.

However, for eager river-gazers there are options. Almost any point north of Beaulieu Estate (North Gate) has open access to the river. The entrance to the National Motor Museum has a bridge across the river and south of this you can easily visit the river and mill pond. The best access point may well be at Bucklers Hard, linked to Beaulieu village by the Solent Way footpath.

I17 Beaulieu's missing monorail

GR SU 385028

There are many examples of light rail in the New Forest and surrounds and Ordnance Survey has, naturally, devised a key to explain them.

Ignoring multiple track railways, the next level down is single track. This is shown as two thin black lines (like a standard fenced track) but with black dashes. A good example of this is square M16. Sidings are shown as very narrow single black lines (see the Military Port in M17).

Narrow gauge railways, or light rapid transit systems (LRTS), are shown as very narrow single black lines with cross hatches. Examples of these can be found at Paultons Park (Q12), Exbury Gardens (G19) and Hythe Pier (would be L19). Interestingly the OS seem to have ignored their own key here and coloured the Hythe Pier stations red rather than yellow, but that's another story.

The monorail at Beaulieu is, fittingly enough, exactly one mile long and was erected in 1974. On the map the north and south stations are shown but the whole monorail track is only shown as a path. The 'path' can be seen looping past the northernmost building (the entrance), entering and leaving the National Motor Museum before sweeping down to Palace House. It then returns north beside the River Beaulieu.

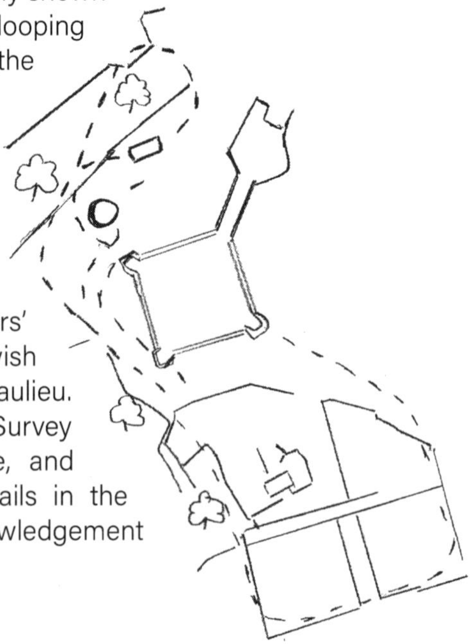

The monorail can be seen fleetingly from outside the visitors' entrance for those who do not wish to visit the attractions at Beaulieu. It is, despite what Ordnance Survey suggests, definitely in existence, and as one of less than ten monorails in the country warrants proper acknowledgement on the map.

118 Beaulieu Gates game

GR SU 400032

The 'three red diamond' symbol is synonymous with the Beaulieu Estate. All of the main entrances to the estate have gateposts marked with the symbol, which is taken from the Montagu coat of arms. It also features on flags or signs on many important or historical buildings.

This particular gate is not marked on the OS map but the gateposts are on a hill top surrounded by Hill Top and Hilltop House, Wood and Farm, so we'll call it Hilltop Gate. The aim of the Beaulieu Gates game is to score as many points as you can by spotting the symbol.

The gates are an obvious starting point; many more points can be earned at Bucklers Hard and in Beaulieu village. The scoring is simple: one symbol equals one point. The target is to score at least 20 points, which gets you the rank of 'Lord of the Manor'.

One fantastic way to get your 20 points is to walk north from Hilltop Gate around the edge of the estate in an anti-clockwise direction all the way to Hatchet Gate and then cut back via Beaulieu village to the start point. This is a walk of around 10 kilometres depending on how many diversions you need to take.

Ranking system:

- 1 point – Village idiot
- 4 points – Village busybody
- 10 points – Smallholder
- 15 points – Craft worker
- 20 points – Lord of the Manor*
- 100 points – Monarch of England*

*You deserve a drink in the Royal Oak, 100 metres from Hilltop Gate.

119 Holbury Manor and Moat

GR SU 428037

The Gothic script on the map will hopefully have banished the notion of a pristine manor house and grounds. What you do find is a good example of a local community caring for an area of greenery on their doorstep.

Warren Copse and Holbury Manor together make up an area of park owned by Fawley Parish Council. The former manor has connections with the monks of Beaulieu and King Henry VIII and a history stretching back to 1180. These days all that remains are signs of former moats and carp ponds. The old mill that would have served the manor is now a lovely secluded pub. The mill pond is a pungent reedbed but the pub is still worthy of a visit.

The amount of wildlife you can see increases the further south into Warren Copse you go. The woodland here is well-managed and you are guided along paths by helpful wooden owls and acorns. A number of real tawny owls have been spotted in the area along with great spotted woodpeckers and song thrushes. Mallards and various gulls visit to the ponds.

Spring may be the best time to visit, as woodland management allows spring flowers to thrive before the tree canopy cuts down the light. Flowers to spot are:

- Celandines: bright yellow flowers with shiny green leaves
- Dog violet: purple-coloured, five-petalled flower
- Primrose: pale yellow with a bright centre, five obvious petals
- Bluebell: blue, and looks like a bell.

122 Ashlett Tide Mill

GR SU 465032

Though less well known than Eling Tide Mill to the north, this mill's location is splendid. Ashlett itself is a tiny community dwarfed by the very small village of Fawley next door. The main buildings in Ashlett are the tide mill, the pub and the former coastguard's house, all sitting beside Ashlett creek and slipway.

Ashlett Tide Mill is fed by a large pond which drains into the creek. The pond itself is outside the park boundary and located right next to the monstrous Fawley Oil Refinery. South of Ashlett are acres of gravel workings and east is the former Fawley Power Station. The creek, with its attractive historic buildings, is an oasis of calm. On a sunny day you can sit on the dock of the bay watching the occasional sailor or simply watching the tide and waiting for the pond to empty.

J4 The best bench in the New Forest

GR SU 179055

Hightown Common is the smallest common owned by the National Trust. It is so small that it is very easy to overlook on the map. In some respects it is typical of the commons found in the north and west of the New Forest. In one respect it is very different.

Below is an 'I Spy'-style check list for you to tick off the highlights of Hightown Common:

Target: 50 points

- Brambles (1 point)
- Oak tree (1 point)
- Robin (1 point)
- Insects (1 point)
- Sedge (2 points)
- Silver birch tree (1 point)
- Heather (1 point)
- Apple tree (2 points)
- Grass (1 point)
- Gorse (1 point)
- Emperor moth (2 points)
- 'Right Honourable George John Shaw Lefevre, Baron Eversley's memorial bench and stone engraving built on behalf of The Commons and Footpaths Preservation Society in grateful memory of their founder and late president. The common was purchased by this organisation with funds subscribed by their members and friends and dedicated to the nation in 1929. The bench was designed by Elisabeth Whitworth Scott, the architect of the Shakespeare Memorial Theatre.'* (45 points; well done).

*Information from plaque located on bench.

J5 Smugglers' Road

GR SU 193055

The Smugglers' Road is easily found these days as a jaunty milestone sits at its junction with the Burley to Picket Post road. The milestone informs us that Ringwood is three miles and Lymington 11 miles away. Lymington may seem like an odd choice of destination to signpost from here, but when the milestone was erected most of the other nearby coastal settlements, beyond the odd fisherman's cottage, did not exist.

In the 18th and 19th centuries both Lymington and Burley thrived from smuggling. Lymington was home to many buccaneers, mercenaries and smugglers as well as being a rotten borough with two MPs. Smuggled goods came ashore anywhere in Dorset or Hampshire where the Revenue could be avoided. Smugglers' roads and New Forest ponies were employed to quickly transport goods inland where they were hidden in pubs, churches or houses. Smugglers were regarded by many as Robin Hood-type figures, helping everyone avoid taxes.

Rudyard Kipling's 'A Smugglers' Song' sums up the situation perfectly. Here is an excerpt:

Five and twenty ponies,
Trotting through the dark —
Brandy for the Parson,
Baccy for the Clerk;
Laces for a lady, letters for a spy,
And watch the wall, my darling,
While the Gentlemen go by!

(https://www.poemhunter.com/poem/a-smuggler-s-song/)

Local tradition has it that nearby Ridley Wood became an open-air smugglers' market when there were goods to sell. Though less lively these days the wood is well worth a visit as part of a circular walk: and you can look to see if any gentlemen go by.

J6 Box Berry Hill

GR SU 207048

According to *www.peakvisor.com, 'Box Berry Hill is a mountain in United Kingdom, with an elevation of 72 metres (236 ft) and a prominence of 6 metres (20 ft) in the England Hills.'* Its parent peak, 'Yr Wyddfa', is better known as Snowdon, 300 miles or so away in North Wales.

If you believe the internet it would appear that any aspiring mountaineer could easily start their career here with a one-minute ascent of one of Snowdon's foothills (footmountains?!). Before you start boasting of your climbing prowess it would be wise to note that in Scotland a mountain is generally regarded as something over 3,000ft (914.4m). These 'Munros' (named after Sir Hugh Munro, who first listed them) also need a prominence of 500ft over surrounding land. On these points Box Berry Hill fails to become a 'Furth', the name given to non-Scottish Munros in the British Isles, such as Snowdon.

A visit to Box Berry Hill reveals that there are no boxes, or even anything resembling a box. There are also no berries (in 2020) or any bushes that might produce berries. However, a hill is defined as *'a naturally raised area of land, not as high or craggy as a mountain'*, meaning that at least the third part of the name is accurate.

Box Berry Hill does provide a nice place to sit and take in the view of White Moor and also to ponder the undulating surface on the hill top.

J7 Burley deer larder and woodcutter

GR SU 230048

In Burley New Inclosure, tucked behind Burley New Cottage, are two attractions just a few metres apart.

On the western side of the track, in the woods around Great Early, is a former deer larder. It's a simple timber building, which is unsurprising as its neighbour is a former timber yard. The building is now used as a base for specially adapted inclusive cycling tours, catering for people with many different disabilities.

In its previous guise it must have been a busy building. There are approximately 2,000 deer in the New Forest, and the park authorities aim to keep this number stable. It is a difficult balancing act: if there are too many deer they cause extensive damage to vegetation, especially trees. Around 30% of the deer, about 650 animals, are culled each year. As yet there are no plans to re-introduce wolves, to keep deer on the move so that they can't overgraze tree seedlings; it would probably create quite a stir!

Keeping an eye on the building from the other side of a track is a wooden woodcutter. This jolly fellow has been carved from a tree trunk and last time I looked he was sporting a yellow safety helmet. Perhaps his role is watching out for any hungry wolves that may be lying in wait for red-clad children visiting the area, or perhaps he is unaware that the deer larder has been emptied.

J8 A bridge for Poohsticks

GR SU 249050

There are many bridges in the New Forest that are suitable for playing Poohsticks. This one has the advantages that you can cycle to it and that there are fir cones and sticks aplenty.

Little did A.A. Milne imagine he was going to change the world when *The House at Pooh Corner* was published in 1928. To briefly recap the story: Winnie the Pooh has a mishap and a fir cone drops into a stream from a bridge. The fir cone is then observed emerging from the other side of the bridge, bringing Pooh his 'Eureka' moment. Christopher Robin, Eeyore, Piglet and Tigger are then introduced to the new game of stick racing, or Poohsticks as it is more commonly known.

Though a simple game, Poohsticks has some rules:

- You need two or more players (this site is suitable for two players only).
- You need to drop your sticks from the upstream side of the bridge.
- Sticks should be of organic material (i.e. not rubbish). Pine cones are acceptable.
- Sticks must be dropped and not thrown.
- Sticks should be dropped on a command such as 'Drop!'
- Competitors need to hasten to the downstream side of the bridge to see whose stick appears first.

There are some additional conventions:

- A picnic is very agreeable.
- Any kind of cheating or manipulation is frowned upon.
- Easily identifiable sticks mean that the winner can be declared more easily.
- The more people, the more fun.
- A summer's day is best.

J9 Blackwater Arboretum

GR SU 265047

The Blackwater Arboretum is quite rightly a popular attraction. There is a large car park opposite with a picnic and barbecue area and usually an ice-cream van. It is also a pleasant though meandering cycle or walk from either Lyndhurst or Brockenhurst.

It is a small site, packed with over a hundred different species of tree from all over the world. There is a leaf-shaped path system but it's best just to wander and wonder. For the best experience try to use your senses as you pass the trees. How loud is the aspen today? Do the different oaks have the same bark texture? Can you believe your eyes when you see the chestnut-leaved oak? Which tree smells most strongly? Note that licking trees is not recommended!

The earliest trees date from the 1850s when Victorian collectors visited all corners of the globe to bring back bigger and better saplings. This one-upmanship has resulted in a wonderful collection of trees which have centuries of life ahead of them.

Although all trees are equal, some are more equal than others, so here is a 'Tree Top Ten' not to miss:

1. – Coast redwood
2. – Turkey oak
3. – Douglas fir
4. – Cherry birch
5. – Japanese cedar
6. – Mountain ash
7. – Snow gum
8. – Western red cedar
9. – Red oak
10. – Chestnut-leaved oak

J10 The Dead Oaks of Drivers Nursery

GR SU 284048

Blocked drainage channels have inundated Drivers Nursery with standing water, killing many of the giant oak trees. This has left an eerie scene, with trees still reaching for the sky but denuded of all small branches and leaves. Work is under way to improve the drainage, so hopefully a new batch of oak will grow to replace the ones currently decaying.

The view here is most stunning during the winter when the surrounding living trees also lose their leaves. Drivers Nursery is unnamed on the OS map but the main viewpoint is from the bridge over Highland Water where the 16m spot height is.

This is certainly a place of contemplation and perhaps artistic inspiration. When observing the scene you may be reminded of a number of famous and not-so-famous paintings. The key ones that stand out are:

- Paul Nash – We Are Making a New World
- Caspar David Friedrich – The Abbey in the Oakwood
- Pieter Bruegel the Elder – The Hunters in the Snow
- Anselm Kiefer – Wald.

J11 Hollands Wood Adders

GR SU 301046

Adders, or common European vipers, can be found all over the New Forest. Their typical habitats include woodland, moorland and heathland and they have been known to take the occasional swim, so the only place you can be confident you won't see an adder is shopping in Lyndhurst.

This area of Hollands Wood features here as it is a mix of woodland and heathland, and is also the former home of the New Forest's (in)famous snake catcher, Harry 'Brusher' Mills. Brusher is credited with killing over 30,000 snakes in the New Forest during Victorian times and was something of a local character. More information about him can be found in The Snakecatcher at Brockenhurst, the former Railway Inn, which was re-named in his honour. In these more enlightened times, of course, adders are a protected species.

The easiest time of year to see an adder is in March when they are warming up after hibernation. Open, sunny areas are their preference, which can mean snakes basking on paths, so be cautious when walking. Adders are very shy creatures and will always try to beat a retreat if they sense humans. The vast majority of bites are inflicted on people who either tread on them or try to pick them up. Though venomous, adder bites are only dangerous to the old, young or vulnerable. That said, bites are very painful and often result in swelling so a trip to casualty is strongly advised.

Adders are recognised by the obvious zig-zag pattern along their backs. Colours vary but females tend to be brown and males grey. Any place where there are lizards, small mammals or ground-nesting birds will attract adders as they regard all these creatures as dinner. Larger adders can reach around 80cm in length though they can seem much bigger when you stumble across them!

If you are not lucky enough to spot an adder on your walks in the New Forest then a visit to the Reptile Centre on the A35 south of Lyndhurst should compensate.

J12 The Frohawk Ride

GR SU 317052, 321051

Frederick William Frohawk is most famous for his mighty tomes *Natural History of British Butterflies* and *The Complete Book of British Butterflies*, published in 1924 and 1934 respectively. Almost a hundred years later these books are still regarded as the definitive guides on the subject.

Frohawk and his first wife spent their honeymoon in the New Forest, famous during Victorian times for its range and number of butterflies. Sadly numbers have declined massively, which is one of the reasons the Forestry Commission established the Frohawk Ride. It was opened in 1996 by Frohawk's youngest daughter, named Valezina after a type of fritillary butterfly. Fritillary butterflies were known as the 'woodman's friend' as they seemed to follow woodcutters, knowing that their activities would bring sunshine and later flowering plants to the new gaps in the forest canopy.

The key to butterfly spotting is the sun. Butterflies love the sunshine and the nectar-laden flowers that depend on it. This means that during the winter the Frohawk Ride is unimpressive; it only comes to life in late April or early May, continuing through to August. Thistle flowers and bramble blossom are the favoured hangout of many fritillaries and 16th July, Frohawk's birthday, is perhaps an auspicious day to visit.

J13 The Bishop's Dyke

GR SU 336053

Bishop's Dyke is written in two places on the OS map and the dyke covers part of squares J13–15. On the ground it is an earth embankment around 1m high and up to 4m wide enclosing about a square mile of land known as the Bishop of Winchester's Purlieu.

The Bishop in question is believed to be John de Pontoise. Hampshire County Council states *'Legend has it that John de Pontoise, Bishop of Winchester, built the bank and ditches around 1284. He was given permission to enclose an area that he could crawl around in a day. To get the largest possible piece of land he spent 24 hours crawling along the ground.'*

(https://www.hants.gov.uk/thingstodo/countryside/walking/newforeststandinghat)

When an area of Royal Forest is enclosed and privately owned it becomes a purlieu. Unless he was a duck fancier or a bog snorkeler, the Bishop could hardly have enclosed less promising land. To the west it is wet; the eastern end is very wet. During wet weather the whole area is completely sodden. Various legends suggest the area was a deer park, a cattle farm or a pond. You can decide which is most likely.

The temptation to circumnavigate the dyke by walking along the top should be resisted. Although the dyke is largely complete, where there are gaps the mire is deep and unrelenting. Many a Duke of Edinburgh's Award group has been caught out by this 'path'. There are many good paths that can be taken from Matley Heath, Beaulieu Road or Pig Bush to see a section of the dyke or to spend several hours exploring the area.

J14 Playstation Ponds

GR SU 344052, 343053, 341051, 340050

If you have used the Playstation games console you will know that there are four control buttons: Circle, Square, Triangle and Cross. This area, in the Bishop of Winchester's Purlieu (see J13 for more information), has three ponds resembling three of those shapes.

The first pond is just outside the north-east corner of the wood containing the 20m ring contour. Unmarked on the map, but obvious on the ground, is an almost perfectly round pond. About a dozen birch trees surround the pond, leaning in from the bank, providing shade for the pond and trying to gain as much access to sunlight as they can. A couple of smaller trees have abandoned the bank and are surrounded by water. Its depth is difficult to gauge but in most seasons the pond remains full.

Less hospitable, due to bog, and trickier to find though it features on the map, is the squarish pond at the end of a line of trees. Its straight lines and the channel running into it show it to be man-made. It is the pond you would least want to picnic next to.

The OS map shows two straight drainage channels flowing from Denny Lodge Inclosure. The northernmost channel now forms a pond of its own. It's larger than either of the other ponds but doesn't yet feature on the OS map. It's triangular in shape, following the geometric pattern of ponds in this square.

Though there are no cross-shaped ponds, anyone wishing to complete the 'Playstation Pond Challenge' can stand at SU 340050. The grid lines here form a perfect cross.

J15 Rowbarrow Pond mire

GR SU 355047

When you visit a mire, make for the viewpoint rather than the destination; here, visit the grid reference rather than Rowbarrow Pond itself. The pond probably takes its name from the bowl barrow (marked 'Tumulus' on the map) that sits 250 metres east of the pond. The 'row' part of the name may refer to the fact that there are additional tumuli to the west, making a row of sorts.

The path from Furzey Brow to the Bishop's Dyke takes you across two 'streams', and from anywhere here you get a great view across the mire. The path has been extensively improved: to slow the flow of water large drainage pipes have been replaced with smaller ones, helping to restore the very rare lowland bog and provide a stunning vista.

Bog restoration has increased the variety and numbers of plants leading to an increase in insects and birdlife. On the negative side naive walkers and ponies occasionally need rescuing when they underestimate the depth of the mire – or, in the folklore version, 'colt-pixeys' lure ponies into the mire by taking the shape of a horse. Similar stories exist across the West Country and in Ireland, where leprechauns and imps take the blame for the foolish behaviour of man or beast.

J16 Gurnetfields Furzebrake monument

GR SU 378052

Despite being close to a number of roads this wonderfully named area of heathland has a wild feel to it. The monument itself is inscribed as follows: 'This stone is erected to mark the spot where S Carter was killed whilst hunting with the NF hounds 116 Jan 1885.' On the rear of the stone is the ominous 'In the midst of life we are in death.' It's an impressively solid piece of stone and easy to find on its promontory.

Gurnetfields refers to the woodland to the south of the heathland. The reason why some areas of woodland are referred to as fields is shrouded in the mists of time. West of the monument, on high ground, are farmland and the Ferney Croft Scout Activity Centre. In all directions are thickets (brakes) of gorse bushes, or furze (fyrs in Old English). North and east of the monument, as the land drops the mires rise. You'd be brave to venture off the path and across the mire, but the rewards of heading in this direction are high – the Beaulieu River is a reasonable size here and it flows through attractive woodland.

J17 Crabhat Inclosure stockade

GR SU 391050

Crabhat Inclosure looks fairly ordinary on the map, though its name does raise a few questions. If the inclosure next door was named after the King's Hat then who or what was the crab, and why did it have a hat? History does not record the answer so you can use your imagination.

Crabhat Inclosure's main point of interest is its great example of a New Forest pound. These can be found dotted around the forest but this one is quite modern and unusual for being sited within woodland. New Forest Commoners, who occupy New Forest land and have rights to graze their animals there, use pounds like this to pen animals for counting, moving or health checking. It's not quite a scene from the O.K. Corral with cowboys and lassos but the New Forest is famed for being sedate.

This particular pen has a plaque with the following inscription: *'Crabhat Pound. This pound is dedicated to Brian Ingram and Don Stephens in appreciation for their contribution to the New Forest. Sponsored by The New Forest Commoners, Defence Association'.* Both men have spent considerable time supporting the rights of Commoners. The New Forest and Commoners are protected by the Verderers, an organisation formed in the Middle Ages to administer forest law on behalf of the King. Their remit in modern times is to protect the traditions and character of the New Forest. The Court of the Verderers is based in Queen's House, Lyndhurst. Decisions made in this building keep the New Forest the special place that it is.

J18 Beaulieu Heath tumuli

GR SU 403051

Beaulieu Heath is a large area extending north east from Lord Montagu's Beaulieu Estate. Most of the area is open-access common land with a number of inclosures to the north.

One thing that makes the area interesting is the number of tumuli dotting the landscape. These ancient burial mounds are sometimes large, sometimes small and occasionally completely overgrown.

One of the best examples is the collection of three tumuli on the western side of Beaulieu Road. Firstly, these tumuli are large – they extend over one hundred metres in length and are higher than all but the tallest people. The tumuli are so high they even get their own contour rings on the OS map. A large tumulus generally indicates that powerful people were buried underneath; three close together often indicates a family. Secondly, these tumuli have their own small moats, which is very unusual in the New Forest. Whether this was an original feature or a later addition is unclear.

A visit to the tumuli, along with a stroll through Dibden Inclosure, makes for a lovely short walk.

K3 Linbrook Almshouses

GR SU 162069

Linford Brook is a small stream that flows down from Milkham Bottom in square M6. When it reaches the ford at Linford it dispenses with part of its name and simply becomes Lin Brook, which gives its name to the almshouses on Highwood Lane.

Almshouses were founded, usually by religious organisations, to house the poor and needy, often local people too old to work. The oldest almshouse still in existence is the Hospital of St Cross and Almshouse of Noble Poverty in Winchester. Founded in 1136 by William the Conqueror's grandson, Henry of Blois, this almshouse is most famous locally for the 'Wayfarer's Dole' – bread and ale for distribution to travellers.

Linbrook's mid-19th-century almshouses are a lot simpler than Winchester's but they are nevertheless Grade II-listed. The listing picks out the following features:

> *'Stone dressings, tilehung gables. 1½ storey, 3 bay with verandah along front. On front 4 thin posts to curly braces to wallplate and similar on inside of wall. Under at LH end and between RH bays plank door under shouldered stone arch. 3 stone 3-light casements. On roof 3 large decorated gabled dormers with paired pointed casements. Roof half-hipped. Ridge stacks between.'*
>
> https://historicengland.org.uk/listing/the-list/list-entry/1302852

A viewing is recommended, followed by a stroll westwards alongside the Lin Brook as it meanders towards the River Avon, taking care not to spill into any of the lakes that flank it.

K4 Linford Bottom

GR SU 180071

If you visit just one stream in the New Forest, this is the one, and this is the best place to see it.

Linford Brook is a good-sized stream here: up to five metres wide and over 50cm deep in places. Meanders create banks and slip-off slopes just like the ones you learned about in geography lessons. In fact, close to the vehicle bridge there is the inevitable oxbow lake. The high banks and beaches also help you cross the brook if you don't want to walk to a bridge. Just make sure you are using the height of the banks to jump from as if you try it in the other direction you are likely to get wet! There are many tributaries that can be explored and allow you to get off the beaten track.

A lot of the surrounding area is grass, so you can picnic right next to the water. Smooth gravel makes the stream bed gentle on your feet and if you look carefully there are occasional deep pools where you could immerse yourself should you wish. On a warm summer's day the whole valley is full of people paddling, damming and picnicking.

At any time of year the walks in the surrounding inclosures and woods are rewarding and for the more adventurous there are cycle paths to Broomy and Bratley Plains.

K5 White-tailed travellers

GR SU 193062

A popular staging post for New Forest travellers is Picket Post Services on the A31. It appears that this has been picked up by white-tailed eagles, with a number of sightings around Picket Post in the last decade. Blashford Lakes and Roe Inclosure, 3km to the north west and north east, have attracted birds and birdwatchers alike.

White-tailed eagles, also known as sea eagles, are Britain's largest bird of prey, with wing spans up to a massive 2.4 metres. Wiped out by hunters and farmers 240 years ago, the last place in England to have a breeding pair was Culver Cliffs on the Isle of Wight. When six of these eagles were reintroduced to the island in 2019 one of the eagles was named Culver. Not long afterwards he paid a visit to the New Forest, spending time in the vicinity of Picket Post. This particular journey took him as far as London before a triumphant return to the Isle of Wight by flying over Culver Cliffs.

Sightings remain very rare but there are plans to bring in more breeding pairs over the next five years. Follow these Forestry England tips for successful eagle spotting:

- Be patient. An obvious statement, but sometimes you just have to be in the right place at the right time.
- Look up when you're out and about. Keep an eye on the sky to make sure you don't miss one if it flies over you.
- Watch other birds. Corvids and buzzards tend to mob an eagle if it's flying low. If the local buzzards are acting strangely, there might be an eagle about.
- Sit and wait at a high point. With a good pair of binoculars or a telescope, you can spot one of the eagles catching the thermals – even at a distance.
- Head out with a friend! It's more fun watching birds with a friend and two pairs of eyes are better than one, especially from a good vantage point.

(https://www.forestryengland.uk/blog/white-tailed-eagle-project-september-2019-update)

K6 Soarley Beeches

GR SU 221067

Soarley Beeches is a small peninsula of soaring beeches jutting out into a sea of mire.

The beech trees are old and some are very bedraggled. One of the largest, towards the eastern end of the spur, measures at least five metres in circumference. The limbs of this tree are plaited together in an extraordinary manner. It's a tree climber's delight – though fallen branches all around might suggest that's not such a good idea.

The ancient oaks and beeches here give Soarley Beeches an air of majesty unmatched by most areas of woodland. The sheer number of fallen branches is testament to their centuries-long battle with the weather. Wind and lightning have wreaked havoc on this exposed hillock but still the trees stand proud.

It is well worth a visit when the winds are light. If you are planning to sit down for a while bring something to sit on as the area is deep in prickly beechnut husks. It's tempting to believe that nearby Soarley Bottom is a reference to this menace!

K7 Stinking Edge Wood

GR SU 226073

Erik the Red's *Saga of the Icelanders*, written about 1000 AD, has this to say about the naming of Greenland: *'In the summer, Erik left to settle in the country he had found, which he called Greenland, as he said people would be attracted there if it had a favorable name.'*

(www.nationalgeographic.com/news/2016/06/iceland-greenland-name-swap)

Whoever named Stinking Edge Wood was clearly not acquainted with the sagas.

Examples of places Erik the Red might have named (if he ever visited the New Forest) would be Redrise Hill, Moon Hill, Camel Green or Honey Hill – all conjure up pleasant expectations. Hag Hill, Spaniards Hole and Jealous Copse are at least intriguing. In terms of negative connotations, Stinking Edge Wood is in a league of its own.

So does Stinking Edge Wood deserve its name? Is it a wood? Yes. Does it have an edge? Yes. Is it stinking? No. The origin of many place names in the New Forest is lost in time. It is possible that Stinking Edge Wood stank in the past. A potential whiffy source would be the substantial bog to the east of the wood, labelled as a braided stream on the OS map. If you were to ignore the path and try to freestyle across the bog, you could be pretty sure to get wet feet and even wet armpits, as New Forest bogs have fearsome reputations to uphold. You could also be pretty sure you would stink, thanks to all the decaying material you would have disturbed. It could well be that Stinking Edge Wood was rather unfairly named by someone foolish enough to try to cross the mire.

K8 A record-breaking road

GR SU 249071

Bolderwood Arboretum Ornamental Drive has a good claim to be the longest street name in the UK. On the Ordnance Survey 1:25,000 map its name stretches over a kilometre and it only just squeezes into the mile of square K8.

A rival for the record is 'Queen Margaret's Road Industrial Estate' in Scarborough. However, at a local pub quiz the correct answer was Bolderwood, and everyone knows the quiz master is always right, even when they aren't. If faced with a choice of driving down one of the two roads then Bolderwood would be a very good choice, unless you are in need of plumbing supplies.

Either side of the narrow drive is ancient woodland, but amongst the huge beeches and oaks are imported coniferous trees – a mix of cedar, fir, cypress and pine, alongside giant redwood. The great size of some of the trees cannot be appreciated from the road; the best way to see the area is to get out of the car and onto the trails that criss-cross the area. Around Bolderwood are a number of marked trails with information boards describing the trees in the arboretum. Walks further south, in North Oakley or Anderwood Inclosures, are equally rewarding and a bit more 'off the beaten track'.

K9 The largest/oldest/most famous tree in the New Forest

GR SU 265065

The Knightwood Oak, also known as 'Queen of the Forest', is certainly the most famous tree in the New Forest. Not many trees have their own car park, trail, protective fence and information boards as well as having the surrounding inclosure named after them. The tree has had famous visitors, including Queen Elizabeth II.

Despite being 600 years old, the Knightwood Oak is unlikely to be the oldest tree in the New Forest; nor is its nearby rival, the Eagle Oak, also about 600 years old. Square H12 in Brockenhurst has a yew that is approximately 1,000 years old, so the only title available to the rivals is 'oldest oak in the Forest'.

With regard to size, the Knightwood Oak is impressive – its branches are the size of very large trees, and its circumference at the base of the main trunk is eight metres and growing, so it is the largest tree in the New Forest. Pollarding (chopping the crown off) the tree in around 1700 has resulted in the trunk splitting into several major parts. Numerous pretenders to the title have been planted nearby – the Deputy Surveyor's Oak, the Millennium Oak and the Queen's Oak (planted by Her Majesty the Queen in 1979) – but it is unlikely that any will ever match the size and fame of this tree.

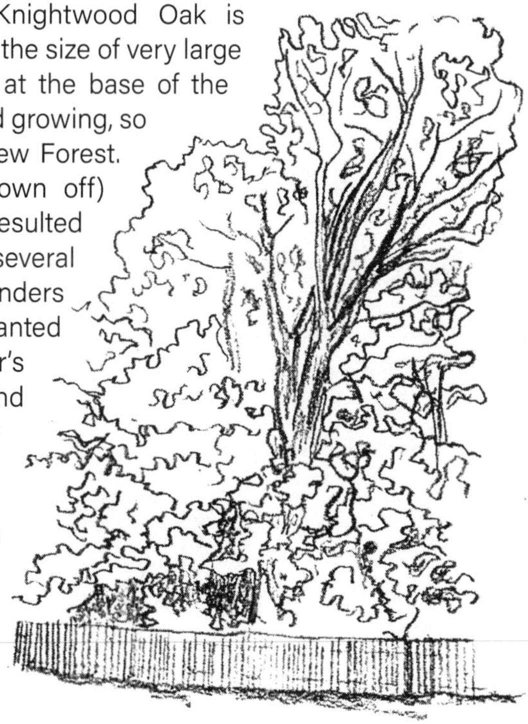

K10 Allum Green House gargoyles

GR SU 279070

The outbuildings of Allum Green House have some of the most impressive gargoyles in the New Forest. It is difficult to date the gargoyles, which adorn what was probably the coach house and stables. A clock tower and weather vane are nice finishing touches.

If the southernmost gargoyle were to take off in the direction of Bramble Hill it would fly directly over a bench with a view of the house. This bench tells a sad story: it is a memorial to four soldiers from the Royal Army Ordnance Corps (RAOC) killed during a Luftwaffe bombing raid. The raid occurred on the night of 5/6 September 1940 and hit the main house where the soldiers were billeted. During the Battle of Britain the number of air bases in the New Forest made it a target for the Luftwaffe as they attempted to annihilate the Royal Air Force. Just a few hundred metres south west of Allum Green hamlet is a series of roadways leading to the Reptile Centre. Though no records seem to have survived, this area looks from the map like a vehicle or ammunition storage area. This was possibly the target of the raid and the reason for the presence of the RAOC.

K11 Philip's Hill cauldron

GR SU 295066

On the OS map Philip's Hill is a promontory leading down from a high point of 53 metres on Pinkney Lane. Why it is marked here, half a kilometre from the 'hill', is a minor mystery. Another minor mystery is why it is called Philip's Hill, but this may be because the hill, along with the Foxlease estate, was owned from 1770 by Sir Philip Jennings Clerke. A well-known soldier and MP in his day, he built an impressive mansion which today serves the Girl Guides. Whether 'Philip' had a great affection for this promontory or perhaps was simply vain may never be known for sure; but vain MPs are not unknown in history.

A further mystery is the cauldron-like area just north of the top of the promontory. It is shown on the map as a pond but is little more than a patch of mud these days. It is a lovely area of woodland and the topography lends itself to den building, tree climbing and general outdoor games. Nearby are further diggings, suggesting the area could have been mined, a theory supported by the name of the area east of Philip's Hill, Brick Kiln Inclosure. Both clay and chalk were needed to make bricks. Though chalk is found no nearer than north Hampshire, Barton clays can be found in the area around Lyndhurst. The pond in nearby Wilverley Park could also disguise a former clay quarry.

K12 Pondhead Inclosure

GR SU 309072

Pondhead Inclosure is a great example of something wonderful being hidden in plain view. Sitting beside Lyndhurst, it is incorporated into the large area of woodland that stretches from Burley, via Brockenhurst, to Beaulieu. On the OS map it looks little different to the neighbouring woodland – mostly deciduous, with a little coniferous. It is also gently rolling open-access land like the neighbouring inclosures.

The main access points are from Beaulieu Road (GR 311076) and various points along Beechen Lane to the south. The first difference you might notice are the high deer fences and gates keeping out unwanted visitors. You will also notice signs showing the area is looked after by the Pondhead Conservation Trust – in fact this area has been protected since Victorian times.

As soon as you step through the gate you will feel the difference in the woodland. All manner of ground vegetation exists that is seldom seen in other inclosures – among the standard oaks and beeches foxgloves, bluebells, nettles and blackberry bushes thrive, along with many types of moss. The reason for this diversity is the work carried out by the Trust's volunteers. Though there is a circular walk, there are also many smaller paths leading through the woodland. Stacks of decaying wood are piled here and there, providing insects with homes and food.

One area is devoted to hazel coppicing. This is done on a ten-year rotation and allows the woodland to rejuvenate. Butterflies are one beneficiary, and the conservation team are actively trying to restore butterfly populations to the area.

Further information is available at www.pondheadconservation.org.uk; but this is an area that really needs to be visited to be understood.

K13 Park Pale

GR SU 324068

The name 'Park Pale' indicates not an area pale in colour but an enclosed area. The earthen embankment labelled Park Pale on the OS map is the boundary of the area. The northern edge follows The Ridge from the 49m trig point near Bolton's Bench; then the Pale heads south and crosses the B3056 into Denny Inclosure before turning west and disappearing in Clayhill Heath. A second section stretches south west to north east from Beechin Lane to the house at Pondhead.

The biggest clue to the purpose of the Park Pale comes from one of the inclosure names within the pale: Park Ground Inclosure. This whole area was previously a large hunting park. The earthen banks and ditches were designed to allow animals in, but not out. Deer, foxes, wild boar and other game could be chased into the pale in advance of a royal hunting party. By the time of the event the Park Pale would be a heaving menagerie of game. Even the most incompetent hunter would have a reasonable chance of hitting something.

Existing on this site since at least the 13th century, the Park Pale also allowed wild animals to be contained in a semi-domestic environment. This meant that during the winter, and other times of food scarcity, meat was easier to access. These days the Park Pale makes a nice walk. In places the earth banks are huge – several metres wide and over a metre high. Elsewhere the structure has disappeared but there are always paths close by to follow.

K14 Beaulieu Road Pony Sale Yard

GR SU 349064

The Beaulieu Road Pony Sale Yard is hidden in plain view opposite Beaulieu Road train station and the Drift Inn pub. A previous incarnation existed directly beside the train station and ponies were often loaded directly on to carriages when sold!

The current yard has existed here since the end of the Second World War, though it was rebuilt in 2002 and extended in 2011 and 2013. It's an impressive set-up and the closest that many of us will get to a rodeo. Wooden pens can hold more than a hundred ponies and evidence of their presence can be seen in spring and summer when wildflowers thrive on the fertilised soil.

The centrepiece is the pagoda-style show ring where Commoners buy and sell ponies raised in the surrounding forest. If you get an opportunity to visit during a sale it's like a cross between the Epsom Derby and a sale at Sotheby's.

Ponies graze the area around the sale yard blissfully unaware of the various fates that may befall them if they are put up for sale. Regarded as placid, hard-working animals, New Forest ponies are often sold to families to start their children on the road to the Horse of the Year Show. One can only imagine how surprised these hardy ponies are when they are moved onto lush grass, with a stable to sleep in!

If watching ponies eat grass has given you an appetite, the Drift Inn has a nice beer garden and a fine selection of food and drink.

K15 Yew Tree Heath trig point

GR SU 362063

From March to July this area is an important nesting ground for breeding waders. This means that the car park is usually closed and the National Park authorities discourage activity. Quietly visiting the trig point here without a dog would cause no issue. In fact, if you stick to the main paths you can hear the twitter of birdsong without causing any inconvenience. An argument put forward by Charles Darwin suggests that any bird daft enough to build its nest on the ground isn't perhaps the 'fittest' in the brain department – bird-brained, perhaps. A counter-argument would be that small birds have a hard enough time dealing with cats, bigger birds and other predators so a bit of peace and quiet after they have given birth is the least we can supply.

The triangulation point gives a reasonable view across Yew Tree Heath and up to Black Down. According to http://trigpointing.uk it was installed on 25 November 1939 and cost £4.11s.3d (old pounds, shillings and pence in case you were wondering). Another fascinating feature of this website is its ranking of trig points. This one is the 5,187th-best trig point in the British Isles. If you were keen to visit the highest-ranking trig point you would need a boat, a pair of stout walking boots, waterproofs, food and a tent. The number 1 triangulation point in the British Isles is on the uninhabited island of St Kilda (Grid reference NA 099000), located over 100 miles off the Scottish mainland in the Atlantic. Maybe the New Forest does not seem quite so remote any more.

K16 A less than trivial group of trees

GR SU 375067

This resembles an oversize Trivial Pursuit 'cheese segment' on the map but is much more impressive in real life. The key feature here is the southern part, shown on the map as boundary, path and strip of deciduous woodland. The boundary is an earth bank, not high enough to stop anything, but clear enough to signify a boundary.

The trees are ancient and deserve more than the two tree symbols on the OS map. There are more oaks than anything else and they are rather majestic. The only rival to the oaks are the beech trees. Beech nuts and acorn cups litter the floor all over the earth bank. Towards the western end there is a beech tree which appears to have been split in three by wind, lightning or gravity. Just beside it is a hollow beech trunk with a perfectly healthy twin growing beside it. Interspersed between the giants are a selection of silver birch, holly and others. At the extreme west of the boundary is a yew tree, standing there like a stranger at the party. It looks like it has been there a number of centuries so perhaps it has been accepted now.

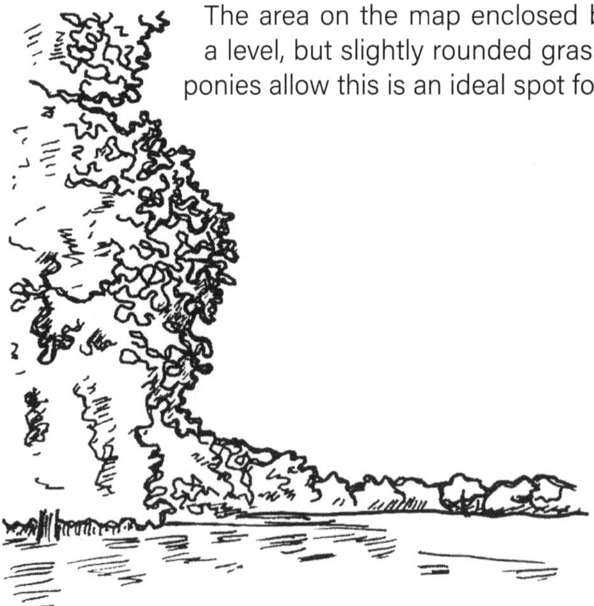

The area on the map enclosed by the tree boundary is a level, but slightly rounded grass area. If the ubiquitous ponies allow this is an ideal spot for ball sports or a picnic.

K17 Dibden Bottom fletching

GR SU 387059

For those who are not archers the term 'fletching' may be unfamiliar. If you look at the map between GR SU 387059 and the footbridge almost directly to the east you will see a water feature that resembles the feathers on an arrow. This represents the fletching-style channels designed to drain the plain north of King's Hat Inclosure.

On a damp day it would not be advisable to pay too close attention to the drainage channels as you will find yourself in a true New Forest mire. During dry periods you can negotiate the area in boots and admire the extraordinary straightness of the drainage channels.

A small stream passes north of the mire before collecting its waters at the road and then travelling a short distance west to join the Beaulieu River.

To the east is a long bridge with a pond beside it. Water and paths from the higher land all around here head towards the bridge. From the bridge, or the higher ground, there are lots of nature-watching opportunities. A large number of deer are often seen in the area though they are fleet of foot and can disappear in an instant. The horses and ponies, also drawn by the combination of water to drink and vegetation to eat, tend to move more slowly.

L3 Rockford

GR SU 164083

If there is time there are two key places to visit in Rockford. Firstly, this small village is home to one of the biggest sandpits in the New Forest. Then, calling at the Alice Lisle pub allows you to watch birds across the Blashford Lakes Nature Reserve from the beer garden – the beer courtesy of a helpful ferret. Confused? Read on.

Rockford Common was previously a quarry, which has left an exposed area of sand on a tall hillside. Leisure activities here are boundless: you could take a short geology lesson or you could just jump on a swing (someone has usually built one) or roll down the sand hill. Further exploration of Rockford Common brings further reward as it is a beautiful area of rolling heathland under the stewardship of the National Trust.

Should you require food or drink after a visit to Rockford Common then the Alice Lisle pub is a good bet. You see on the OS map that the pub was almost consumed when Rockford Lake was a gravel pit. This lake now provides a great opportunity to birdwatch or simply enjoy the large beer garden.

A newspaper cutting displayed in the pub reveals how a local customer's ferret, Fred, saved the day following a pub refurbishment. Engineers could not find a way to get the beer lines from the cellar to the bar until Fred stepped up to the mark, and with a rope tied round his neck crawled through and found a route. This allowed the lines to be pulled through, meaning the pub could re-open on schedule and people with sand-filled shoes could get a well-deserved drink.

L4 Water Slade Bottom

GR SU 176077, 179080

Slade is the old English word for a small valley, and here, in the midst of a small pine stand, springs the water that this valley is named after. In dry weather the word 'spring' might overstate matters as this is more of a seepage mire; however if it has been wet the word is apt. It is odd to see a 'baby's head bog' in this kind of setting and crossing it is far more of a challenge than walking around it.

A small stream quickly forms and drains into a pond as it reaches the boundary of Waterslade Farm, located here due to the water source. The next place you can pick up Water Slade stream is at the southern end of the farm's boundary. On its short trip down the valley it has increased in size and importance. If you walk along the western fence you have a super view of the valley and stream.

The first thing you encounter when visiting the stream at the southern end of the farm is a large and boggy pond. Closer inspection reveals an earth dam approximately 10m across, 1m high and 2m wide. Though not large, the dammed pond is quite an unusual find in the New Forest and very popular with ponies, birds and other creatures, great and small.

L5 Castle Piece

GR SU 199089

Castle Piece is an earthwork much like other forts and lodges across the Forest. It's a large example and almost perfectly round. The bank varies from around 5–15m wide and 1m high and moss carpets a section cut out for a track. What is lovely here is the woodland. Trees are a mix of deciduous and coniferous. Ferns and flowers cover the floor.

Castle Piece holds a special place in my memory as it was here that my eyes were opened to the New Forest's ancient history. In my teens I had walked and camped all over the New Forest. In my twenties I spent time working at the Motor Museum at Beaulieu and cycled a lot around the Forest. By my thirties I was a Duke of Edinburgh Award leader and was supervising groups of students in the New Forest.

During that time a colleague took a group of us to Castle Piece and explained that the banks we were looking at were built around 2500 years ago. The idea that people had lived here in a small stockade astounded me; even more impressive was that evidence of their lives still survived. Further stories involved hunting lodges and rutting deer and a whole new aspect of the New Forest was opened up to me. It is partly thanks to Ian Coppack, now the landlord of the Scott Arms in Kingston, Isle of Purbeck, that this book was written. If you should visit the Isle of Purbeck please drop in and say hello to him.

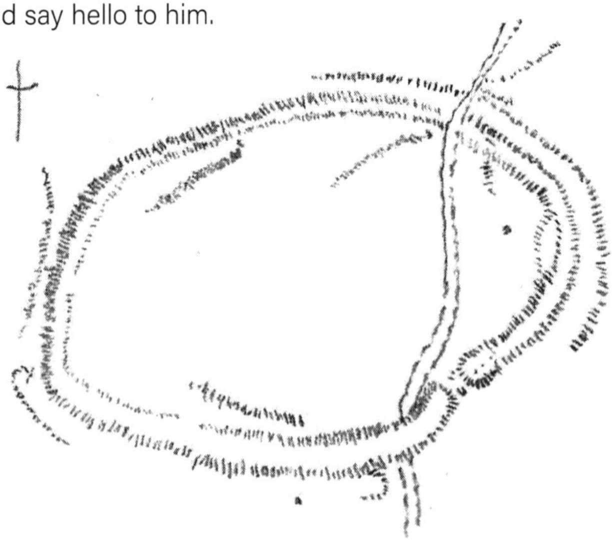

L6 Advice from John Richard de Capel Wise

GR SU 222087

In 1862 de Capel Wise published *The New Forest: its history and its scenery*, and one delightful paragraph reads:

> 'Let no one, however, think they know anything of the Forest by simply keeping to the high road and the beaten tracks. They must go into it, across the fern and the heather, and, if necessary, over the swamps, into such old woods as Barrow's Moor, Mark Ash, Bushey Bratley and Oakley, wandering at their own will among the trees. The best advice which I can give to see the Forest is to follow the course of one of its streams, to make it your friend and companion, and go wherever it goes. It will be sure to take you through the greenest valleys, and past the thickest woods, and under the largest trees. No step along with it is ever lost, for it never goes out of its way but in search of some fresh beauty.'
>
> (Google books: The New Forest - Its History and its Scenery)

All of the places he mentions are in the vicinity of Bolderwood Arboretum Ornamental Drive and three are now heavily forested. The fourth, Bushey Bratley, is almost certainly the area renamed Bushy Bradley on modern OS maps. On the map it seems that some time over the last 150 years the name has been corrupted to Bradley.

De Capel Wise did not have to contend with the A31 but if you take his advice and follow the course of the stream you soon leave the traffic behind. Bushy Bradley starts as a grassy bog, fed by a small pipe and with a fence to discourage venturesome souls. The grass is interspersed with bracken and heather, and birdsong soon begins to replace the noise of the traffic. Trees also begin to take over, starting small but as the valley widens the trees get taller. If you're taking the valley floor route, water shines back at you ready to swallow your foot if you misstep. You can follow this stream all the way to Burley Lodge or, if time allows, all the way to Lymington.

L7 Log weirs on Bratley Water

GR SU 235079

Much of the New Forest has been heavily influenced by humankind. In the area around Bolderwood there are numerous introduced ornamental trees, for example, many of which are awe-inspiringly large. Paths and bridges, to allow easy access to the woods, are also obvious examples. For centuries, agriculturalists aimed to drain water from the land, and in many places it is clear that the water channels have been manipulated – especially where you see dead-straight channels.

The log weirs here are an example of the re-evaluation of that drainage policy, for a number of reasons. Drainage of mires reduces biodiversity and is no longer encouraged. Fast-flowing water in straight channels results in flooding downstream, due to the shortened lag-time. Another consequence is increased erosion; water travelling quickly has more energy. Some of the erosion is directed at the banks, producing the infamous oxbow lakes of geography-lesson fame. Erosion also removes gravel and larger stones from the riverbed, producing deep gullies.

Log weirs slow the stream down, allowing sediment to build up in the pools and reducing further erosion. Nature produces its own log weirs but formerly these were regarded as obstructions and cleared. The soothing ambience of these log weirs encourages adults to sit down and relax. The effect on children is generally less tranquil as the weirs can easily become an adventure playground with very wet consequences.

L8 Bolderwood Deer Sanctuary

GR SU 241085

The Deer Sanctuary here is a real honeypot site with lots of visitors and an ice-cream van in all but the worst weather. Rangers feed the deer most afternoons in the summer so deer spotting should be simple (though not guaranteed). The Sanctuary is easily accessible and a good destination for those with limited time, mobility or patience.

However, there are deer all over the New Forest, and it is great to bump into them as you turn a corner in the woodland, or spy one that has not noticed you. Below is a simple guide to the types of deer that live in the New Forest. Just remember that they usually spot you a long time before you spot them.

Fallow deer were introduced by the Normans and are the most common deer in the New Forest. You are most likely to see them in herds in deciduous woodland; they are easy to spot as they have a lot of spots. When they are running away you can see their white rumps with a black line running from top to bottom.

Roe deer are native to the UK and relatively common in the New Forest. You are most likely to see them in woodland or nearby fields. In size they resemble small sheep, and they are usually found in small groups. When running away you can see their plain white rumps.

Red deer are the largest mammals in the UK and are capable of injuring people or dogs so be cautious. Red deer are reddish-brown with off-white rumps and are typically found in woodland. The older males, with large antlers, are a particularly impressive sight.

Sika deer are related to red deer but only arrived in the New Forest in 1902 when Lord Montagu was gifted a pair by King Edward VII. Not content with life on the Beaulieu estate, a number eventually escaped, settling in the Beaulieu and Brockenhurst area. They look similar to fallow deer but have a black spot above their white rump.

Muntjac deer are rarely seen in the New Forest. They are the size of a smallish dog, with long back legs and a brown rump. Males have very simple antlers and they are usually solitary.

L9 The Portuguese Fireplace

GR SU 265077

The Portuguese Fireplace is an odd sight as you walk or drive by. In an area with trees in almost every direction, a stone, brick and concrete fireplace sits on a grass lawn. Over two metres tall and almost as wide, the fireplace is tiered like a wedding cake. The front is inlaid flint with a brick arch around the hearth; the rear is concrete. Ponies often pose artlessly for photos.

A former plaque (missing in November 2019) used to say: 'This is the site of a hutted camp occupied by a Portuguese army unit during the First World War. This unit assisted the depleted local labour force in producing timber for the war effort. The Forestry Commission have retained the fireplace from the cookhouse as a memorial to the men who lived and worked here and acknowledge the financial assistance of the Portuguese government in its renovation.'

No mention is made of the Canadian lumberjacks who ran the camp and worked with the Portuguese; however the Canadian government did not assist financially with the renovation! Perhaps they could pay for a new, reworded plaque.

The camp was very large with dozens of buildings. Around Millyford Bridge, on both sides of the road, are numerous concrete foundations of the former huts. One set of remains resembles a series on Tetris blocks: squares, rectangles and L-shapes.

L10 Cut Walk

GR SU 289081

This is a wonderful way to visit some of the best ancient woodland in the New Forest. Cut Walk follows the route of a road constructed in 1725 at the request of the Lord Warden of the New Forest. It is little more than a path now, but the surroundings are spectacular.

Cut Walk starts beside the A35 at Swan Green, a grassy hill that doubles up as a cricket pitch in the summer. After a few hundred metres you have the option to climb the 93-metre Lyndhurst Hill and visit its mound and unimpressive reservoir. At this point cartographers will notice they are on the south-eastern peak of a classic saddle feature. To the north west is James's Hill, also 93 metres high, and sporting a small pond. In the saddle between the two peaks someone in the 18th century was kind enough to build a pub, aptly named The New Forest Inn (like many others).

Returning to Cut Walk the woodland is undulating with a few open areas and plenty of water features. The brick-built 'Roman Bridge' is nothing of the sort but an attractive bridge in its own right and a good spot for playing Poohsticks. Shortly after this, at Warwick Slade, the walk meets the A35 again. To turn this into a circular walk carefully cross the A35 (there is a subway at GR 278066) and head north east via the homely hamlet of Gritnam and vibrant village of Bank. You'll notice on the map that Bank has a pub, the Oak Inn, which is very highly recommended. A further pub, The Swan, sits beside the A35, opposite Swan Green.

L11 The source of the Beaulieu River

GR SU 294089

Just as the Nile is the world's longest river whereas the Amazon is the largest by volume, two New Forest rivers contend for the title of 'best'. At 22km long, the Lymington River might be 6,628km shorter than the Nile but it is still 2km longer than the Beaulieu River; however, where Beaulieu River is the champion is in terms of breadth. Thanks to the tidal nature of its lower third it contains a lot more water than its westerly neighbour, though a lot less than its very much more westerly neighbour the Amazon. In past times this hydropower ran the mill in Beaulieu village.

Bearing in mind its claim to be the best river in the New Forest you would expect a more auspicious source, but in fact the River Beaulieu starts in the garden of a cottage in north Lyndhurst. This is private land but within a few metres a trickle makes its way through a tunnel under the road and forms the boundary of a small green. Still underwhelming at this stage, the stream comes to life between the A337 and A35.

Though still small, the River Beaulieu starts to show a bit of its character as it bounds the New Forest Golf Club surrounded by trees and crisscrossed by footbridges. By the time it reaches the wonderfully named Dunces Arch, and flows under the A35, it has become the kind of stream that is fun to follow.

L12 Bolton's Bench cricket ground and surrounds

GR SU 307080

It is truly flummoxing to try and choose the highlight here. There seems to be something for everyone.

Within 500 metres of the cricket pavilion are several points of interest, the first of which is the pavilion itself. Half mini-Tudor mansion, half thatched cottage, it nonetheless blends in with its attractive natural surroundings.

East-north-east of this is a small chapel and cemetery. As with many ancient cemeteries, the trees alone are worth a visit. To the east is a simple trig point, coincidently marking the start of a walk beside the Park Pale. This partially encloses a large area of woodland to the south of the square and makes for a splendid walk.

Below the trig point is another Lyndhurst highlight. The Pit (disused) resembles a giant sand dune and is a giant playground on sunny days. If you do not mind people kicking sand everywhere the south-facing aspect of the dune allows you to soak up the rays and imagine you are on a beach somewhere exotic.

A Victorian stone water trough lies on the path from the sand pit to the cricket ground. Carving on the trough boldly proclaims 'A merciful man is merciful to his beast'.

Lastly we arrive at Bolton's Bench. An ancient yew tree surrounded by a circular bench sits on a small hill. This gives you a good opportunity to look back at the places you've visited and take a deserved break.

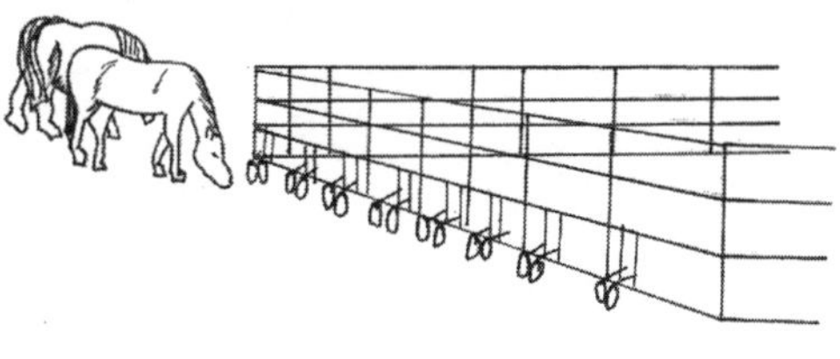

L13 Row Hill

GR SU 320084

Surrounded as it is by bog in most directions, getting to Row Hill can be an adventure. Some of the bog comes and goes with the rain. The OS map is very optimistic, excluding a lot of damp ground and saving cartographers adding lots of blue tufty symbols. Realistically, all the forested areas around here are marshy and the blue lines for streams on the map simply represent bog. Nearby Fox Hill has a field surrounded by drainage ditches, creating an area which is a little less wet than its environs.

The 'rows' are also on a grander scale on the ground than they are on the map. There are several rows rather than two, extending from the line of trees to the west up to the top of the hill.

These rows are simply large earth banks, the highest around three metres tall. They are dispersed amongst ferns and birch trees, making for a wonderfully calm and relaxing spot. The only sounds you hear are birdsong, the wind in the trees and possibly your own squelching socks depending on your choice of footwear.

Old maps reveal the origin of the rows.

> *'In the 1870s, the 6" to the mile OS map offers a little more information, and highlights one of White Moor's military associations – a Volunteers' Rifle Range which is also shown in 1898, complete with Marker's Hut, Flagstaff and Target, but not in 1909.'*
>
> (www.newforestexplorersguide.co.uk)

So it appears that the rows were in fact shooting butts until the turn of the last century. As the area was full of troops during the First and Second World Wars it could well be that the rows were returned to their original use before soldiers moved off to France. Row Hill is certainly more peaceful and less dangerous in 2020.

L14 Matley Holms

GR SU 341079

Matley Holms is a large area of grass and heather very popular with cattle, ponies and deer. On a sunny day, with the right light and a good imagination, the grazing herds and grassland resemble a less exotic version of the Serengeti. Gazelle, zebras and buffalo are present here but the giraffe and elephants are missing, along with top predators (thankfully).

Penning the area in on the north and south flanks are Fulliford and Matley bogs. These tree-lined, slow-moving streams offer drinking water for animals but are very boggy in places and provide a natural barrier to animals and man alike. The streams join at the railway and within a couple of kilometres form a fast-flowing River Beaulieu. It is hard to imagine these sluggish, muddy waters becoming part of a majestic river.

Matley Wood in the west provides shade on sunnier days under ancient oak and beech trees – a typically pleasant piece of woodland. The type of heathland found in Matley Holms is internationally rare: in fact, according to the New Forest National Park Authority, 'the New Forest has the most extensive area of heathland remaining in Europe (over 10,000ha)'. Matley Holms, with its flora and fauna, is a great place to enjoy this type of landscape.

L15 Longdown starfish decoy site

GR SU 358086, 362084

Longdown and Denny Lodge were sites for the mysterious starfish decoy project during the Second World War. When the Luftwaffe bombers switched from airfields to cities Southampton became a prime target – as well as being a major port Southampton was also where the Spitfire was built. After extensive bombing of the Supermarine factory over the period of 24–26 September 1940, 'shadow' factories – small workshops scattered across Southampton, Hampshire and Wiltshire – were opened to continue production, and to protect the city decoy sites were built close by.

The aim of the decoy sites was to simulate a burning city and tempt Luftwaffe bombers away from their intended targets. Trenches filled with flammable material soaked in paraffin or oil were lit when bombers were detected. The Denny Lodge site also had a light decoy system which attempted to recreate a poorly blacked-out city.

Originally called 'Special Fire', or 'SF', sites, the decoy site near Bristol became known as 'Starfish', and the name was adopted for all the decoys.

LiDAR surveys have been completed at both sites to identify the starfish structures and any bomb damage. Denny Lodge appears undamaged but Longdown shows some evidence of attack. Finding this evidence on the ground is more difficult. The area around the grid reference is undulating, which could indicate the remains of craters; however, 80 years on it is difficult to say for sure. There are a couple of long scars in the ground which could also be linked. Longdown Inclosure is a nice area for a walk and you can let your imagination do the work. Just south of the area is the appropriately named Decoy Pond Farm.

L16 Fox Hill

GR SU 370080

Fox Hill has surprisingly good views for such a small hill. A good viewpoint is important to any animal that needs to keep an eye out for prey or for the hunter in human form.

To the south lies Ipley Inclosure wood which links up with the main bulk of the wooded New Forest via the Beaulieu River. Covered ground like this provides protection from predators and allows creatures to range in search of food. A lack of cover across the New Forest's many heathlands, due to constant grazing by deer and Commoners' animals, means that all forms of small mammals, such as voles and mice, are few in number.

To the north is flat farmland, easily accessed from the hill and ideal for smash-and-grab raids. Any rabbits, rats or hedgehogs crossing this land may catch the beady eye of a fox.

Fox Hill itself has a sandy soil which allows for easy digging of burrows (or more correctly earths). Foxes often find their dinner underground though the soil in the New Forest has a low earthworm content. Another fox-sized snack is the dung beetle – very common due to the amount of dung deposited by grazing animals.

The chances of spotting a fox on Fox Hill (or anywhere else) are quite low as they are shy creatures. Highly-developed eyesight and hearing mean they will most likely sense you first. Fox droppings are a good indicator of their presence though. Foxes mark their territory frequently and conspicuously. The droppings usually contain fur, feathers and even beetle wings.

L17 All Saints' Church – A joyful resurrection

GR SU 397085

All Saints' Church in Dibden is one of several All Saints' churches in the New Forest, but this one holds an unenviable national first. According to the local newspaper, the *Southern Daily Echo*, on June 20, 1940 it became the first church in the country to be bombed in the Second World War.

Its location close to Marchwood military port, combined with the poor navigational skills of the air crew, were the first problem. The next issue was the church's isolated location, coupled with overworked and inexperienced fire-fighters. The result was that the church was almost gutted. The roof and windows were completely destroyed and the walls badly damaged. This was one of the first large raids on Southampton Water – later in the war bombing was better targeted and fire crews were much more experienced.

First recorded in 1262, All Saints' Church was not re-consecrated until 1955. A plaque inside simply states: 'The Parish Church of All Saint's, Dibden was destroyed by enemy action on 20th June 1940 and restored 2nd April 1955. A joyful resurrection.'

For nearly 15 years the church sat forlornly and uselessly at the end of its lane, but there's another sad tale nearby. When you visit the graveyard, spare a thought for the trig point positioned on the small hill behind the church. Marking a paltry 31-metre hill, in the middle of a field with no public access, it is destined to sit unvisited and unused for eternity. Perhaps if visitors to the church view it through the holly bushes it will represent a joyful confirmation.

L18 Modern defences using dykes

GR SU 407087

Associated British Ports (ABP) own approximately 3km^2 of land directly adjacent to the New Forest, between Marchwood military port and Hythe. The site was initially constructed using material dredged from Southampton Water in 1967. Large, flat and next to the water, it was perfect for a possible future port expansion. Large, flat and next to the water, it was also perfect for wading birds, thousands of whom took up residence. When ABP decided they wanted to use the land to extend their port operations the Battle of Dibden Bay ensued. Fought initially in council chambers the battle ended up in Parliament where transport minister Tony McNulty vetoed the £600 million project. Local residents, councils, MPs, environmentalists and birds rejoiced while ABP retired to lick their wounds.

If the land had been included in the New Forest National Park when it was established in 2005 local birds and residents could sleep comfortably knowing the Site of Special Scientific Interest (SSSI) was safe. However ABP made sure this did not happen, so there could be a second Battle of Dibden Bay.

The dykes here are of both ditch and levee varieties. They lie directly adjacent to the park boundary, next to a public footpath. Together with a fence and aggressive bushes they form an impenetrable obstacle, breached here and there by gates.

At the southern end of the ABP-owned land is the interesting Hythe Marina (a few metres outside the park boundary) and Hythe Pier and Railway. Pier fans will delight in the fact that it is the oldest pier railway in continuous operation in the world! Non-pier fans might think it's a little shabby. However, it provides access to the Hythe Ferry to Southampton, or just a cheap and cheerful way to view Southampton Water.

M3 Huff-duff and the ginger tomcat

GR SU 176104

Ibsley Common is a dramatic location, seeming far higher than its paltry 77m height on the map. To the west you can catch views of the River Avon and in all other directions the woodland seems to be confined to low-lying areas. In fact Ibsley is surrounded by 'bottoms', including the impressively-named Great Bottom. Little wonder, then, that when they needed to build a top-secret direction-finding station (DF station) during the Second World War they chose this high, remote location.

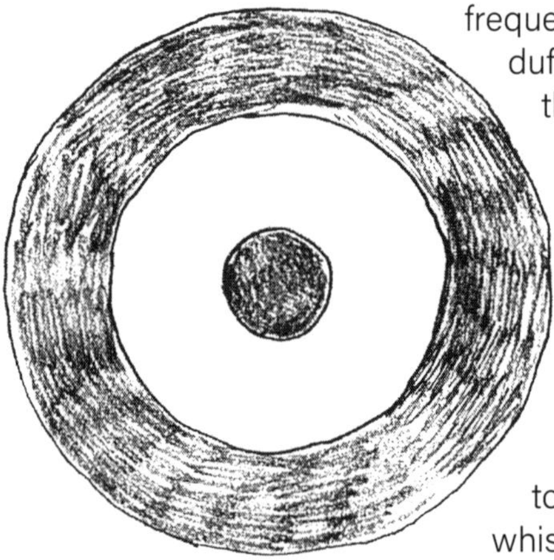

The DF station was later upgraded to a high-frequency direction-finding (HFDF, or huff-duff) station, which played a vital role in the war locating and directing Allied aircraft. RAF Ibsley had an additional secret weapon in the form of a ginger tomcat. The adopted cat loved the warmth of the radio transmitter and would spend most of its time stationed there. The crew soon realised that the cat picked up signals before they did, so started to watch out for twitching ears or whiskers. The cat is credited with having contributed to the saving of planes and pilots.

Much of RAF Ibsley has disappeared but an octagonal blast wall marks the spot where the main wooden control tower used to be. Surrounding the wall are 16 concrete blocks indicating compass points. A hundred metres away are the remains of the crew's accommodation and an air raid shelter. More details, including about our feline hero, can be found on information boards at both sites.

M4 Linwood Bog adventure walk and Nature Reserve

GR SU 178096

For the most adventurous experience this spot is best entered through the small re-entrant (valley) in Great Bottom. There is a right of way marked but no real path across the very boggy ground. If you have an older map the extent of Linwood Bog is massively understated and wellington boots are highly recommended. The path from the west is slightly better and there is an even more prudent path from the south.

The Nature Reserve itself is described by the Hampshire and Isle of Wight Wildlife Trust (HIWWT) as follows:

> 'The woodland reserve, a gift from Gladys Haines, is a mixture of oak, birch and beech glades with areas of wet heath and meadows, beside the Dockens Water. This rich blend of habitats has created perfect conditions for a variety of wildlife. Special wildlife: In late spring and early summer, enjoy the profusion of wildflowers including marsh thistle, violets, wood sorrel and wood sage.'

Except for permit holders, access to the Nature Reserve is restricted to the right of way. Casual visitors will be happy with the view from the dilapidated boardwalk but permits are available from HIWWT. This is a very small reserve which affords protection from human interference to both flora and fauna, so visits away from the footpath should ideally be minimised.

M5 Shepherd's Hut

GR SU 198106

In a small wooded field, just up the track from the High Corner Inn, sits a delightful example of a traditional shepherd's hut. Most shepherd's huts are on glamping sites and will cost you a fortune to investigate – you can look at this one for nothing. There is no public access to the field but views from the track are perfectly sufficient.

A small stained-glass window adorns the rear of the hut, in a section of green galvanised corrugated iron. The rest of the hut is painted metallic grey or light rust-coloured. The front appears to be made of wooden slats; deer antlers add a local feel. The wheels and towing hitch all appear to be in working order and a chimney pokes up through the roof. Inside there would traditionally be a stove for cooking and heating, a bed and a seating area.

Fans of Thomas Hardy's *Far From the Madding Crowd* will be reminded of farmer Gabriel Oak's shepherd's hut. Shepherds needed to be in close proximity to their sheep to protect them, help ewes give birth and move the sheep from pasture to pasture. In the eighteenth and nineteenth centuries shepherd's huts were very common but they fell out of favour in the 1950s as farming practices changed. Hopefully this hut has many years ahead of it as a photogenic curiosity.

M6 Linford Brook

GR SU 218100

Linford Brook is a delightful stream once it gets going. Though its source, on the east side of Milkham Inclosure, gives little hint of what is to come it is worthy of investigation. Exploring the tributaries that start in Milkham or Buckherd Bottoms is a full-on adventure: waders, a raft and an emergency beacon are all recommended. A pair of wellingtons should suffice for this adventure, which is just a couple of hundred metres from a car park.

Without wellingtons this crossing can be quite a challenge on damp days. The grass pathway gives way to mud and then shingle. The stream can be either a dribble or several steps across but the shingle bed is firm.

Trying to traverse to the east is not a good idea. It's an old-fashioned New Forest mire here, with 'baby's head' tufts of grass on the edges and deep enveloping bog in the middle. Every kind of bog plant and insect seems to be contained within just a few metres.

Traversing west is similar but with a stand of oaks beside the stream. A few oaks have given up standing and act as slippery bridges. The rest of the oaks are in stark contrast to the conifers that dominate this area. There's also a narrow spot where jumping might be the best option.

Once you've crossed Linford Brook you need to decide how to celebrate your success. A walk to the trig point at 104 metres promises firmer ground. Following the Brook continues the adventure.

M7 The Underpass Chalybeate

GR SU 240106

A chalybeate is a spring that contains iron minerals; famous examples include Royal Tunbridge Wells and Harrogate. This particular chalybeate is unlikely to enjoy fame or royal patronage as it lies just a few metres from the A35. If you approach it from the south, it starts in the dip and continues to the underpass entrance.

The rusty colour of the water and soil is caused by the oxidation of iron minerals such as siderite and pyrite. These have been washed out of the sandy soil around Spreading Oak that sits on top of a layer of clay.

According to William Addison, in the 1840s chalybeate waters were, *'reputedly good for worms, colic, the melancholy and enriching the blood; it was suited to the treatment of the vapours, killed flatworms in the belly, loosened the clammy humours of the body and dried the brain; it could also make the fat lean and the lean fat'*

(www.malvernwaters.com/nationalparks.asp?search=yes&p=7&id=307)

I would strongly recommend you not to try the waters from this particular chalybeate, especially if you are already unwell! In a similarly unscientific way chalybeates are also thought to cure mange in dogs, and in some areas have picked up the name 'dog wells'. If your dog is thirsty and has mange it might be worthwhile encouraging it to have a little drink.

M8 Canadian Memorial

GR SU 240092

The Canadian Memorial sits just a few yards from a car park on the edge of Highland Water Inclosure. It's a poignant site and well worth a quick visit.

The memorial is surrounded with a wooden fence to keep out hungry ponies. The focal point is a simple wooden cross flanked by the Canadian and Union flags. A plaque explains the reason for the memorial:

'On this site a cross was erected to the glory of God on 14th April 1944. Services were held here until D-Day 6th June 1944 by men of the 3rd Canadian Division R.C.A.S.C. [Royal Canadian Army Service Corps]'.

Thousands of Canadian troops were based in the New Forest in the build-up to D-Day. The men who attended services here were some of the 14,000 Canadians who stormed Juno Beach in Normandy. They were supported by 10,000 Canadian sailors and 15 squadrons of planes. They suffered over 1,000 casualties, including 359 killed, on the first day.

Friends and relatives of soldiers who fought in the Second World War often leave personal tributes and Canadian flags, poppies, crosses and wreaths. The Canadian Memorial is a place to take a few minutes to think about what extraordinary sacrifices people make for others.

M9 Hart Hill trig point and bench

GR SU 261102, 262101

Although triangulation has been replaced with aerial photography and digital mapping, the network of trig points remains, and Hart Hill hosts possibly the most redundant trig point in the New Forest. At 104 metres this is one of the highest in the Forest. However, any unlucky surveyor trying to pick out points to triangulate with would be sorely tested: the furthest you can see from the Hart Hill trig point, deep in vegetation, is around 50 metres.

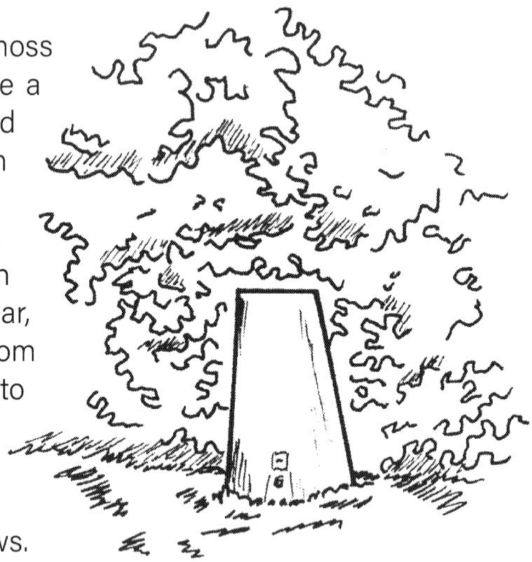

From its mossy grass base, moss climbs up the trig point. There are a variety of lichens on the top and sides, though sadly no map lichen – rhizocarpon geographicum is found in cold, mountainous areas, so not Hart Hill. A birch tree, with almost the girth of the concrete pillar, grows beside the trig point. From two sides holly trees threaten to embrace it whilst in the summer ferns threaten to obscure it. Most of the hill is covered in a variety of trees, restricting any views.

However, just a little way down the track to Wick Wood is a bench put in place so you can admire a view. A plaque explains that *'the seat with a view'* was placed here in memory of Dr Arthur Burnett, his wife Louise and their eldest son, Dr James Burnett. Further plaques are in memory of two other sons, Major General John (Bunny) Burnett, CB DSO OBE MC, and Dr Peter Burnett. A family that gave so much service to their community and country are still doing so with this fine bench.

> *'Rest awhile and reflect that we who are living can enjoy the beauty of the countryside.'*

M10 Minstead woodside boundary

GR SU 273101

Minstead village has been in existence since before the Domesday Book, in which it was listed as Mintestede. This meant 'mint place', as wild mint grew in the area. A 'manor', in the form of a hunting lodge and later a military camp, has existed here for over a thousand years. In 1719 a traditional manor house was built and the woodland and gardens around it established.

The wooded area around Minstead Manor is remarkably well-protected from accidental encroachment. There is a one-metre-plus bank topped with beech trees interspersed with holly. Just to be sure, behind this is a fence with a maze of jumbled rhododendron bushes at the back. In winter, conifers are visible. Badgers appear to respect no boundary and there are a number of holes in the earth bank. This area has one of the best examples of this type of historic ditch and bank boundary, common to medieval estates.

A little further south, around GR SU 278095, is a section of 19th century metal estate fencing. This is another type of boundary which is becoming rare. A combination of the buildings, boundaries and character of this area has led to the whole Stoney Cross to Emery Down region being declared a conservation area within the New Forest.

M11 Fleet Water Mill Pond and dam

GR SU 295100

The names Mill Lane, Mill Pond and The Mill House all lead to an obvious conclusion. The only thing that is out of kilter is that Mill Stream runs 300 metres to the south, and the mill is fed instead by Fleet Water. The source of the Beaulieu River is also close by but runs south rather than east.

The positioning of the public right of way means there is only limited access to the Mill Pond. However you can gain a good appreciation of the pond and how large it is. The banks are covered with a mix of trees, supporting a wealth of hidden wildlife.

The earth dam that restrains the pond is sizeable, around 50 metres long and 8 metres high in places. Between the dam and the track is a primeval-looking bog. This bog, and numerous water outflows, drain under the track via a series of brick bridges. The first two (most southerly) outflows are fairly run of the mill but the third is more impressive. On the east side of the track is a ravine perhaps unrivalled in the New Forest. The current flow along this ravine gives no clues as to how it was formed as most of the water now flows along the fourth, most northerly channel. The water has a spring in its step here, as it heads toward the tide mill at Eling, around 10km away.

M12 Ironshill

GR SU 316099

Often the clue is in the name. In an otherwise fairly typical area of woodland sits an otherwise fairly typical hill. If you have cycled here you would have needed to change gear and if you were walking you might have loosened your jacket zip. Other than that it is a pretty inconsequential hill. The views are not great due to the number of trees but we've established that there is a hill.

So what about the iron? A little detective work is needed to work out the link. A geological investigation of the soil here reveals it to be a mixture of Barton and Becton Sands (similarly found at Bolton's Bench) and Barton Clay. The same combination occurs at Hengistbury Head, just south of the New Forest and Christchurch.

Hengistbury Head is famous for its ironstone doggers, 1–2-metre lumps of ironstone formed within a larger clay/sand sedimentary layer. The sea eroded the softer rock below the doggers causing them to drop down to beach level, where they helped protect the cliff against erosion by absorbing the force of the waves. This worked well until people realised you could get good-quality iron ore from the doggers and carted them off, leaving the cliffs exposed.

It looks like a similar fate befell the ironstone of Ironshill as there are numerous old workings, resembling an abandoned trench system. The consequences are less spectacular – Christchurch is liable to be inundated if Hengistbury Head is breeched – but it shows that the land has a story to tell.

M13 Ashurst Wood Railway Bridge

GR SU 335094

There are many railway bridges in the New Forest. When the railway was first built it divided areas of grazing land as well as many tracks and roads, ancient and new. Bridges and tunnels mean that you never need to walk more than a kilometre in order to find the nearest crossing point. This benefits both man and beast and helps prevent wildlife attempting to cross elsewhere.

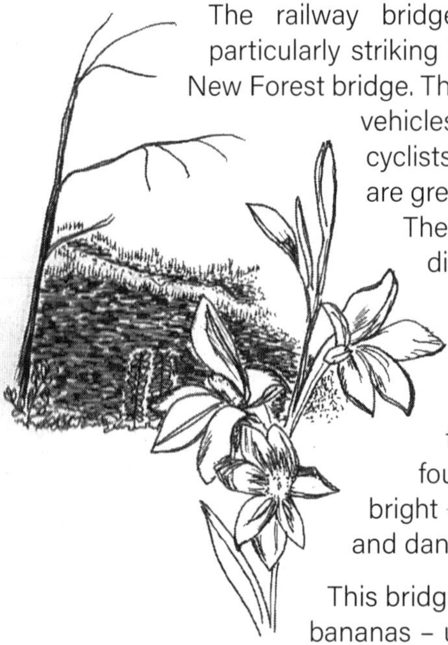

The railway bridge adjacent to Ashurst Wood is not particularly striking but is a good example of a fairly typical New Forest bridge. The track it services is only used by forestry vehicles, which share it with pedestrians and cyclists. On both northern sides of the bridge are great examples of boggy New Forest ponds. The water is a special kind of brown that dissuades all sane people from entering. Trees and various damp-loving plants grow around the ponds so despite appearances they are rich in wildlife. In this spot, and similar spots around the New Forest, the yellow iris can be found flowering in May and June. It is a bright and joyous flower to find in such a dark and dank place.

This bridge has brick-built supports in the shape of bananas – using their concave structure to hold the earth and gravel in place. Many New Forest bridges have railings to prevent people from viewing the railway below; in this case they have been replaced allowing almost unrestricted views up and down the line. Trainspotters will find the selection of trains a little dull on a normal day but when a special train is due this is a great viewing point.

M14 Royal Hunting Lodge (site of), Churchplace Inclosure

GR SU 342096

There are many sites of royal hunting lodges in the New Forest. This should come as no surprise given the New Forest's past. One of William the Conqueror's priorities after settling in was to organise an area to go hunting, and the New Forest suited his purpose admirably. It was close to his capital in Winchester, the farmland was generally poor and there was a good mix of forest and heathland to support game.

'Nova Foresta' (from the Norman French for New Royal Hunting Ground) was established in 1079. Forest Laws were introduced to protect the pigs and deer of the forest as well as the vegetation that was their habitat – vert and venison; vert meaning 'green' and venison from the Latin and Norman word 'to hunt'. Forest Laws were harshly enforced, with punishments including blinding, the chopping off of hands and even death. For the selfish amusement of himself and his court Duke William had inadvertently protected the New Forest in a way that has allowed it to survive to today. Local residents were not impressed at the time as their sources of meat were now off-limits.

Sadly the last 1,000 years have not treated the wooden hunting lodges well. Though the lodges are long gone, their sites remain. This particular site is one of the more impressive. There is a small, man-made earthen hillock atop a small hill. All around are soaring oaks and beeches, holly and ferns cover the forest floor. Standing beneath these majestic trees it does not take a great stretch of the imagination to rebuild the lodge and picture a royal hunting party.

If you happen to pass Church Place Cottage (GR SU 341103), pause to admire the somewhat macabre deer's bust on the outside of the building.

M15 Barker-Mill Estates cottages

GR SU 359092

On Deerleap Lane are a matching pair of three-house terraces, or trito-detached or even trient-detached houses if you prefer. The style and quality of the houses is impressive, with architectural and aesthetic consideration given to every aspect, from the ridge tiles to the windows. Further north on Deerleap Lane, near the junction with Hunters Inn Hill, are another three houses (N14) and on the A35 on Spicers Hill are a trio of trios (in the theorectical square N15). All the houses are very similar with only subtle differences, such as unusual glass-tiled roof windows on the porches of some houses but not others.

The obvious question is, who built such pleasant, harmoniously designed houses on the very edge of the traditional New Forest? The answer has its roots in the 16th century, when a Sussex man called John Mill moved to Southampton and became a wealthy merchant. So successful was John Mill that his family crest adorns the medieval Bargate in the centre of Southampton. John and his descendants shrewdly invested in land, buying thousands of acres beside Southampton Water and along the River Test. As well as acquiring land, through the years the Mills collected names, becoming Barker Mill and at one stage Vaudrey Barker Mill.

In the eighteenth century the Mill family inherited and remodelled Mottisfont Abbey (now owned by the National Trust) and are also believed to be responsible for planting at Mottisfont the UK's oldest and largest surviving London plane tree. As well as Mottisfont, a lot of Barker-Mill land was sold off over time. Land at Millbrook became Southampton's container dock and Millbrook and Lordshill council estates. The new Ordnance Survey HQ was also built on former Barker-Mill land.

These attractive estate houses are a reminder that the Barker-Mill charitable foundation still has a lot of land and influence in the Ashurst and Colbury area of the New Forest. It is refreshing to see that the cottages are not painted in 'estate' colours such as the gaudy yellow that distinguishes the houses of the Cowdray estate in West Sussex.

M16 Marchwood train station

GR SU 383101

Unless a lot has changed you will not be able to catch a train to Marchwood train station. In fact, nobody under the age of around 50 will have been able to do so. This is because in 1966, a few months before England hosted the football World Cup, this branch line was closed to passenger trains.

The train station still exists in reasonably good condition, as does its platform. The highlight here is the level-crossing signalling. Gantry signals are in place on both sides of the road but the signals on the south east are most impressive. The gantry itself is pretty rudimentary but the two stop/go signs are splendid. They are from a time when things were designed for form as well as function, probably dating from the 1920s when the station was opened. Functionally there is a light with two filters to indicate stop and go. The filters are different shapes – one oval, one round. There is a red and white semaphore signal arm that is also used to indicate stop and go, designed so that in the event of a mechanical breakdown gravity would drop it to the 'stop' position. You would be very lucky to see the semaphore signals in anything other than the closed position as the only trains that use this branch line are for the nearby military port.

The latticework posts are both functional and attractive but the highlight is the swirled point at the top, resembling a First World War German helmet. Perhaps, in these more environmentally enlightened times, this branch line will be reopened, perhaps . . .

M17 The railway to nowhere which defines LARGE and SLOW

GR SU 393093

This single-track railway does of course lead somewhere, it's just that it is no longer used. Passenger trains stopped travelling this line in 1966 but it was another 50 years before the last train left Fawley Oil Refinery. In the intervening half-century trains regularly carried petroleum products along the Hythe and Fawley stretch.

Public footpaths from this small crossing mainly lead to the barbed-wire-topped fence surrounding the military port. If you have an interest in fences or want to spy on the trains parked in the port area you have several options. Another (generally muddy) path takes you all the way to Hythe Village Marina via L18.

A sign at the crossing is particularly informative if you ever wondered what a LARGE or SLOW VEHICLE is:

LARGE means over 61'6" (18.75m) long or 9'6" (2.9m) wide or 44 tonnes total weight. SLOW means 5mph or less.

It is unlikely the dozen houses in this cul-de-sac are ever visited by LARGE or SLOW vehicles and as there are no trains running it's questionable whether the drivers would take the time to phone for permission to cross.

N3 Gorley Hill

GR SU 164111

Gorley Hill, or Gorley Common, is not as common as it sounds; in fact it's rather unusual. It has very steep flanks on all sides except the north: ideal for a defensive position. The OS map marks it as a 'Fort', indicating that it fulfilled precisely this role in the past. On the 1945 OS map it is a 'Camp'; but the idea is the same. There is evidence of an Iron Age defensive position at the southern end of Gorley Hill. Views from here across the Avon valley are superb.

The stream on the southern flank resembles a moat but it is too small to dissuade all but the most inappropriately shod. Huckles Brook has a selection of bridges and fords and is worth a visit in its own right.

Once you get to the top of Gorley Hill you find it is almost as flat as a tabletop, within a rim resembling a high defensive wall. All of this is entirely modern, and the result of large-scale gravel extraction in the 1950s and 60s. The 1945 OS map shows a rounded spur at Gorley Hill, so it has effectively been decapitated. Though flat, Gorley Common is surprisingly interesting. It has an open feel with some gorse and silver birch; larger trees are restricted to the steep slopes.

N4 Disappearing rights of way

GR SU 181114

Nobody likes losing their rights and that is exactly what appears to be happening on the OS map to Ogden's Purlieu. Four rights of way seem to enter a type of Bermuda triangle; they disappear as you walk away from the direction of the River Avon. On Rockford Common a further four green dashed paths disappear, though the path is still marked as continuing on the map.

On 24 April 1924 ramblers and communists staged the 'Mass Trespass of Kinder Scout' in the Peak District to secure access to open country for walkers. Thankfully this does not need to be re-enacted in the New Forest: the 1925 Law of Property Act means that both walkers and horse riders have the right to walk or ride on Crown Land anywhere in the New Forest, and for historical reasons this covers most of the National Park.

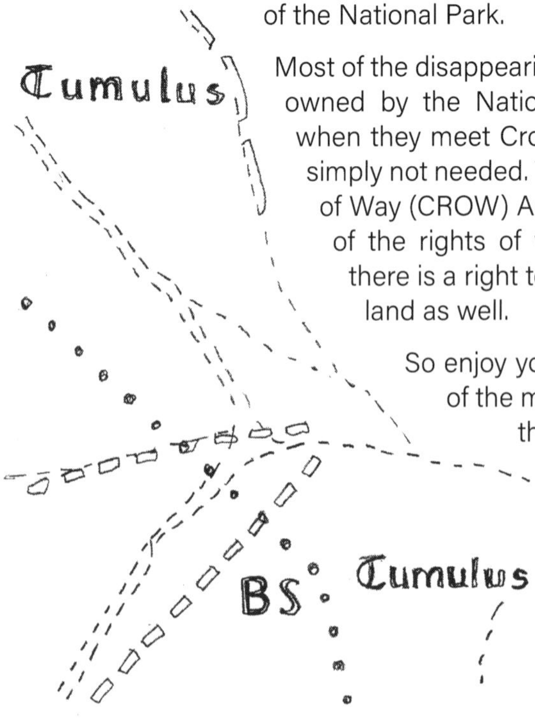

Most of the disappearing rights of way are on land owned by the National Trust and they vanish when they meet Crown Land because they are simply not needed. The Countryside and Rights of Way (CROW) Act of 2000 means that most of the rights of way are now irrelevant, as there is a right to roam on most non-Crown land as well.

So enjoy your right to roam over some of the most wonderful landscape in the British Isles.

N5 The geological secrets of Hasley Hill

GR SU 193123

Visitors to the Great and Little Witches (named after two unequally-sized spurs) of Hasley Hill will have noticed the change in colour and consistency underfoot. Sands vary in colour from white to rust brown. If anyone has visited Alum Bay on the Isle of Wight they might be reminded of the Needles Sand Shop where you can fill glass containers with up to 21 shades of local sand.

Aside from the sand are numerous flint gravels, most common to the east of Hasley Hill. Occasionally a rarer rock will appear, often exposed by badgers or foxes digging holes. This rock, varying from dark to milk chocolate in shade, is called heathstone. Information about this interesting stone can be obtained from Dr Ian West's very informative website: www.southampton.ac.uk/~imw/New-Forest-Geology-Guide.htm#contact-Ian.

Heathstones, iron-cemented sandstones, are found across Hampshire and Dorset. In acidic areas, common in many parts of the New Forest, a podzol soil can form. A podzol soil is characterised by an infertile, ash-coloured layer above a more nutrient-rich red or brown layer. The result of this here is a washed-out looking upper layer, shown by lighter-coloured sands, and an accumulation of irons in a hard layer lower down. Heathstone is one of the only hard rocks found in the New Forest and is suitable for construction; indeed Studland Church in Dorset is built from heathstone. It is possible that some of the larger holes in this area (on top of Great Witch for example) are actually the result of quarrying heathstone.

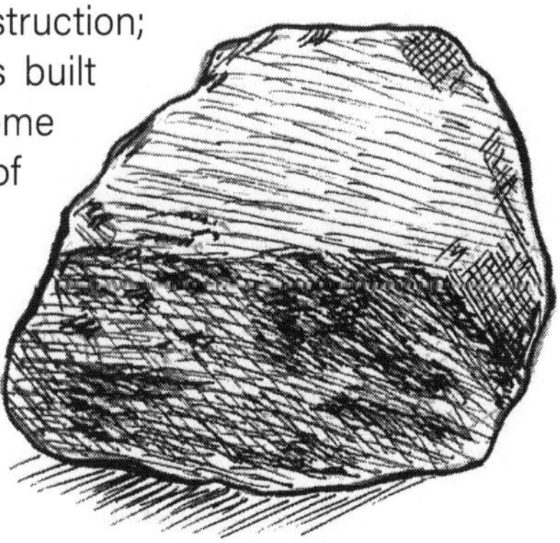

N6 Broomy Pond

GR SU 211107

Broomy Pond is a place for ponies, photographers and picnickers. Do not be fooled by the much smaller and less photogenic pond beside the track to Broomy Lodge, though this one is fine for the ponies. Photographers and picnickers will want to position themselves on the grass to the south-west side of the pond. Any adventures downstream will quickly reveal why there are five marsh symbols shown here on the OS map.

The pond itself is fairly attractive with reeds and white water lilies. White water lilies flower between June and August and produce Britain's largest flowers as well as a home for a multitude of insects and amphibians. The surrounding heather adds a lot of colourful interest when it flowers, between July and September. The key to a great photo here is to capture the trees of an inclosure in the background.

The origins of the pond are a bit of a mystery. It is clearly man-made and shelters all manner of wildlife. Broomy Lodge itself, but not the pond, is shown on the 1811 OS map. The key difference between that map and a modern one is that Broomy Walk is writ large across the area between Milkham and Broomy Inclosures. In 1967 the OS map shows no pond, but by 2006 it has appeared on the map, albeit unnamed.

N7 Ocknell Pond

GR SU 234119

The clay soil in this part of the New Forest has led to the formation of a number of ponds at just over 100 metres above sea level. Ocknell Pond has a long history, unlike its upstart neighbour Cadman's Pool, which was dug in the 1960s. The local story is that Arthur Cadman, the Deputy Surveyor of the New Forest, dug it to 'enhance the scene'. He succeeded in this and Cadman's Pool is now very popular with ducks, ponies, deer and people.

The history of Ocknell Pond goes back around 1000 years. It is said to be the place where in 1100 AD Sir Walter Tyrell washed King William Rufus' blood from his hands after his regicide/unlucky accident. As with all good tall tales there is a twist in the tail: the pond turns blood-red just once a year. If you are unlucky enough to visit Ocknell Pond on another day, just remember the words of Macbeth: 'Will all great Neptune's ocean wash this blood clean from my hand? No, this my hand will rather the multitudinous seas incarnadine, making the green one red.'

In more recently documented history, during the Second World War Ocknell Pond was part of Stoney Cross Airfield. Old aerial photographs show the pond surrounded by aircraft hard standings, similar to the ones in square N8. Evidence of the airfield is all around, indeed the road from Janesmoor Plain was the site of the main runway.

N8 Stoney Cross Airfield's famous visitor

GR SU 250120

The New Forest has long been popular with visitors. Many of the early visitors were royalty and Queen Victoria was known to have been keen to buy Eaglehurst (G22) before settling on Osborne House on the Isle of Wight. In 1946 the US Army Chief of Staff (later President) General Dwight D. ('Ike') Eisenhower, after sailing from New York to Southampton, flew to Germany from Stoney Cross. The Stoney Cross he visited is very different to the one you see today. It was flat then, as now, but all around was the bustle of a busy airfield. If you stand at GR SU 250120 and face southwest a large area of aircraft hard standings, now a campsite, is the largest remaining evidence of the airfield (and the funkiest-looking on the map). All around Ocknell Pond were more hard standings. In wartime, the whole of the area of heathland to the south of Ocknell Pond was filled with accommodation for servicemen and women.

The road between Cadman's Pool and Janesmoor Pond follows the route of the main runway, which allowed planes to take off into the prevailing wind. A second runway ran north–south from just west of Janesmoor Pond and a third ran parallel to the road down to the A31. Janesmoor Pond was another site of hard standings and more buildings were to be found around the current site of Long Beech campsite. Ike's plane departed from a spot opposite the campsite, currently two car parks, where there was a large concrete area ideal for parking large aircraft.

For a circular walk idea see square O8 (clue below).

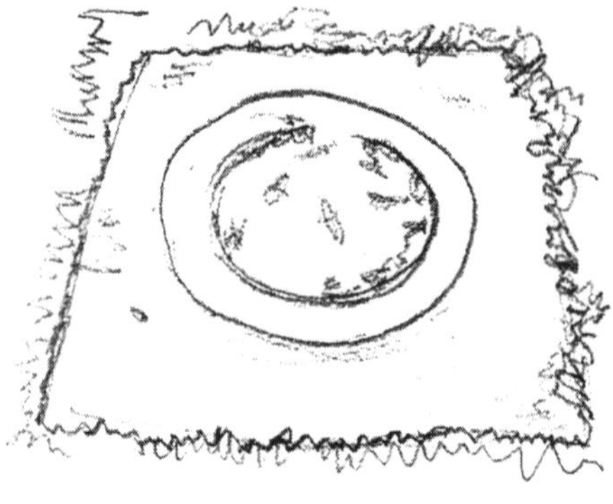

N9 Dams and bridges

GR SU 270111

Most of the woodland to the south and west of Minstead is privately owned with little public access. This is a little island of open access woodland with paths from the eastern and western tips.

The key feature here is probably the stream junction crossed by a series of bridges/boardwalks. It's a really clear stream despite a huge amount of leaf litter in the autumn. Fallen trees create small waterfalls along both arms of the stream and these are well worth exploration. If you want to cross just use the nearest fallen tree as a bridge. Despite the obvious drainage there is a lot of mud in all but the driest conditions.

The woods are mixed coniferous and deciduous but clear and open for the most part. Within short distances the woods change character but it is a small area so you can explore without fear of getting lost. If you do feel lost just head downhill till you meet a stream and follow it.

Trees have fallen or been felled in a higgledy-piggledy manner everywhere: this is a great spot to find a walking stick or a wood sculpture. Watch your footing as any trip will send you into the nearest mud-puddle. Dens and games of Poohsticks are options for less mature visitors of any age.

N10 Minstead

GR SU 281110

Minstead Village Green is tiny but packed with interest. A chestnut tree planted to celebrate the Silver Jubilee of King George V and Queen Mary takes pride of place on the green itself. Surrounding the tree is a circular bench providing sun or shade, as you prefer.

A war memorial stands next to a covered well on the western side of the green and the flag of St George flies above them. Just beside the flagpole, on the road leading to the church, is another interesting building. Minstead Technical School has a plaque announcing: 'This room was erected AD 1857 on a site presented by H E Compton Esq of Manor House to commemorate the 60th year of the reign of Queen Victoria.' It is now a private residence, but the plaque shows the respect accorded to skilled trades in Victorian times.

A short distance up the hill is a delightful 13th century church. Here, under a large tree, is Sir Arthur Conan Doyle's grave. Perhaps of more interest to youngsters would be the stocks on the village green. Originally designed as a punishment for wrongdoers, these stocks were installed in 2002 when Queen Elizabeth II celebrated her Golden Jubilee. Adults might be tempted to put aside sinful thoughts and visit The Trusted Servant pub instead. It's an imposing building and hosts regular beer festivals. The stocks probably get a lot busier during festival time.

N11 The Eling-Minsteel boundary

GR SU 294121, 294120, 296113, 297107

There are a series of boundary stones, marking where one manor's estate finished and the next started, in this square. The oldest is from 1750 and the most modern from 1822. The stones have various inscriptions, with the most puzzling being 'Minsteel'. This must be a corruption of Minstead, which has had a boundary with Eling since before 1066. However there is no record of Minsteel being used so perhaps it is simply a 'Ye olde typo'.

Visiting one stone would be sufficient to 'tick the box'; however for more competitive readers there is a points system. The maximum is fifteen points, though five points should be regarded as sufficient. Points, based on how easy or hard the boundary stones are to find, are awarded as follows, from north to south:

BP1: 2 points

BP2: 5 points

BP3: 0 points, as it is mostly buried and next to the main road. 1 point instead for visiting Brockis Hill

BP4: 4 points

There are three bonus points for anyone who finds the one square metre of tiled ground at GR SU 297106. 100 bonus points are on offer for anyone who can find out why a Victorian-style red, cream and black area of tiling should feature in Furzy Lawn Inclosure.

N12 The worst cricket ground in England?

GR SU 309111

Bartley Cricket Club players are a hardy bunch. Whether you are a cricket aficionado or blissfully ignorant of the game you'll be surprised by this cricket ground.

We'll start in the middle and move outwards. The wicket is quite good compared to the rest of the pitch but quite poor compared to any school or local park ground. Bumps and an interesting incline make bowling and batting an unpredictable experience.

As you move away from the centre the ground becomes considerably worse. Bumps are replaced by lumps and trip hazards abound for anyone foolish enough to look up for a flying ball. The fence is evidently not doing its job as manure is plentiful and the ground gets boggier the further out you go.

The boundary is especially unorthodox. In cricket the boundary is generally circular, ensuring it is equidistant from the wicket. It is usually marked with a thick rope or a painted white line. Here we have a large square with first a drainage ditch, then a line of silver birch trees and finally a wire fence. Which one of these barriers the ball needs to cross to score a four or six is unclear. Either way fielders have to be very careful of getting wet or being wiped out by a low branch.

A reasonable-looking club house sits a little way outside the boundary next to an ancient oak. The woodland here is old and teeming with birds. Though the quality of the cricket ground is poor, the nature around Great and Little Stubby Hat, to the west, is wonderful.

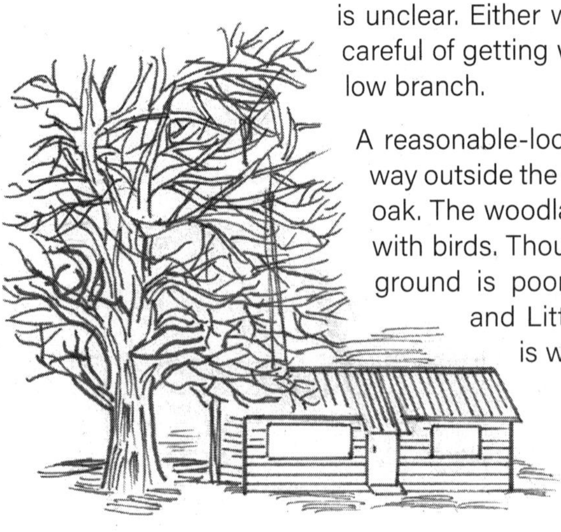

N13 Great and little gables

GR SU 325122, 318114

The village of Woodlands has a wonderfully eclectic selection of outbuildings and houses. Highlights start with the Nissen huts on the north side of Rossiters Lane at Ridge Farm and the lovely old open barn opposite. From here to The Gamekeeper pub on Woodlands Road and beyond are countless architectural gems. One house has drooping-eye windows, another has a porthole; there are cute thatched cottages and gateways, an errant milestone which needs to be seen at number 222 and the pub itself is interesting for its short stature.

When Woodlands Road turns south the footpath opposite passes what could be the smallest house in the New Forest. It has a front door and a well-formed roof, but only one window, which takes up most of the frontage. It also appears to have been built by someone ill-disposed to getting wet – to provide the householder with shelter a metre-wide strip is missing from the front of the house. When your house is the size of a small caravan a porch might have been a better alternative; but perhaps rather than housing a person made of sugar, it is an ornate and over-engineered shed. Back on the road, at the neighbouring larger houses are a small but fabulous collection of outbuildings, resembling a mini-Skansen.

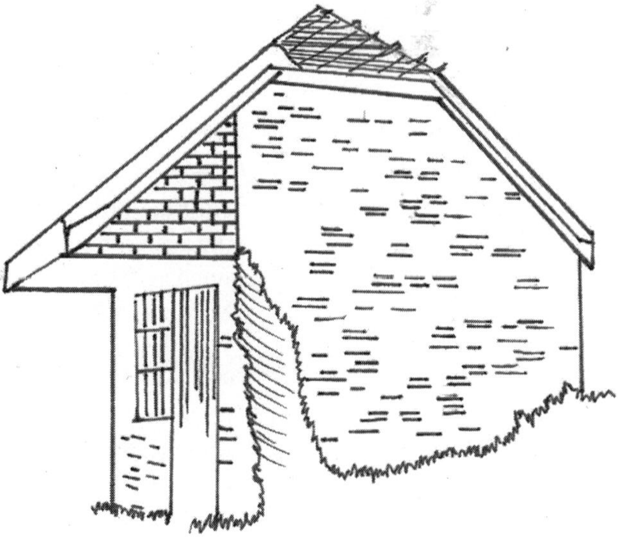

N14 Bartley Water

GR SU 341118

Bartley Water has virtually no interest in arriving at the sea. Starting as Ringwood Ford Bottom at 100m above sea level it descends to the sea over 11km as the crow flies. In reality the river must travel close to 50km as it meanders to avoid the end of its journey. Near the source of the river it becomes the Mill Stream and then gets held up at the man-made Leominstead Pond. After crossing under the Emery Down road the meandering really starts. At this point a parish boundary follows the river for a period. Bartley Water keeps the cartographer busy here, adding dots to indicate the boundary until just after the A337. Here the boundary heads north to join another waterway. Cartographic relief is short-lived, though, as this stream becomes a tributary of Bartley Water and it dawdles its way past Little Stubby Hat and Yewtree Hill. The parish boundary comes and goes but at the site I've chosen it is back, along with a footbridge and a public right of way.

The river is in its full meandering splendour here, tree-lined and cutting through a number of fields. Another smaller stream also joins here and both branches are crossable using the lazy trees lining the bank (at a slight risk). The trees here seem as disinterested at reaching for the sky as the river is to conclude its journey to Southampton Water. Many of them lurch close to horizontal across the water. If you're coming from the level crossing you'll hopefully notice that it has a step in the middle. I'm sure this is not a unique feature but it does mean you have to tread carefully while watching for trains bearing down on you.

After the A326 most of Bartley Water is accessible by footpath. Another couple of kilometres eastwards and the reasons for the river's lack of drive are revealed. Firstly, there is the tide pushing against the flow. Secondly, there is a tidal basin where water is stored for Eling tide mill. Why rush when you will only be put to work? Lastly, there is the embarrassment of being the cause of a toll on motorists – car drivers might expect a far larger bridge and river for £1. The Itchen bridge in nearby Southampton costs only 60p but is 28 metres high and close to 1km long. However, both the bashful Bartley and the illustrious Itchen soon meet in Southampton Water and travel together to the Solent.

03 Spring-fed blackberries

GR SU 173125

Hyde Common is a small area of heathland that slopes down from Frogham in the north. Along the 70- and 75-metre contour lines are a series of springs and wells. There are seven shown on the OS map within a kilometre from east to west, plus additional ones dotted all around.

The most famous is Abbots Well and Spring, dating from at least 1217. Less famous are the seepage springs that sit on the hillside above Ogden's Farm. These are not the bubbly springs with gushing streams you might find in mountainous areas; as the name implies, water seeps out of the ground creating an area of bog. The reason for the springs here is the transition of the bedrock from Barton Sand to impermeable clay. These beds are named after Barton on Sea, where the cliffs expose the alternate clay and sand layers very clearly.

There are many more springs than the map suggests, so ample opportunities to get your feet wet. As you descend the hill via the bridleway you will notice the gorse bushes giving way to brambles, and in autumn there are plenty of berries to be picked. It seems that slow-moving spring water is ideal for cultivating copious, flavourful blackberries. There is a suggestion that blackberries are another superfood; they certainly contain large doses of vitamins C and K, to compensate for any scratches you get from the brambles.

04 The view from Hampton Ridge

GR SU 188136

The car park at Abbots Well is shown on the map as a viewpoint. The view from here is good and you can quickly visit the Abbots Well spring too. Just a short walk away the view is even better. Climbing Hampton Ridge takes you to the giddy heights of 100 metres and a trig point to celebrate. An additional 300 metre walk brings you to an odd site and a wonderful view.

Slightly to the south of the track and just before a significant bend is a very large arrow. It is made of concrete blocks set into the ground and measures around 10 metres across and 30 metres long. It is not a typical New Forest sight. However, if you look in the direction the arrow is pointing in you will see one of the best views there is: the panorama of Thompson's Castle (a spur), Latchmore Bottom and then the Great and Little Witches (more spurs) in front of Hasley Hill. There are almost always animals grazing in the area and the height means the sky feels 'big'. The 50-metre drop into the valley is quite steep for the New Forest and any wind will make it atmospheric.

So who is responsible for this giant arrow that points to the one the best views in the New Forest? As with many things, it is almost certainly just a coincidence that the Air Ministry decided to build an illuminable target indicator on this spot. The arrow was simply to show aircraft the direction of the target when Ashley Walk was a bombing range. De Havilland Mosquitoes dropped bombs where cows now graze and passing walkers are plagued by mosquitoes.

05 Latchmore Brook in Alderhill Inclosure

GR SU 202131

Latchmore Brook has its source at Picket Corner, approximately 115m above sea level. Though that does not sound very impressive as a national or international statistic, it is most likely a New Forest record. Nearby Pipers Wait is the (likely) highest point in the New Forest at 129m, and it has the only other contender for highest stream source, with Shepherds Gutter flowing east through Black Bush from around the same height. However, this square is far from the 'highlands' and involves a more mature Latchmore Brook.

You can pick up this attractive stream at many points in Amberwood or Alderhill Inclosures, though the southern end of Alderhill is less impressive. It is best to use the smaller paths right next to the water on either bank.

Following the stream at any time of the year is pleasant but in the spring, with the sun shimmering off the water, it is mesmerising. You can spot small fish, in the deep pools shaded by the trees, and a wide variety of birds and insects. There are often deer in this inclosure although any loud noises are more likely to come from squirrels busily burying or digging up nuts and crashing through branches.

Many fallen trees lie across the stream giving those who can't wade or jump options for crossing. Alternatively you could use the bridges which cross Latchmore Brook at irregular intervals. As it is a reasonable distance from any car park a picnic next to the stream is highly recommended.

06 The Churchyard

GR SU 210125

Many royal hunting lodges date back to medieval times and are often shown on maps with a reference to churches. There are a number of theories as to why this is. One (now discredited) idea was that the Norman kings razed villages, including their churches, when they turned the New Forest into a hunting ground. Another theory is that the areas around the royal hunting lodges resembled the grounds of a church due to the ancient oaks, beeches and – particularly – yews. Most have earthworks resembling the boundary or outline of a building of importance.

The Churchyard is probably the best example of a former royal hunting lodge in the New Forest and to find a church amongst the trees would not be a surprise. This area of woodland has a very large number of ancient yew trees amongst holly bushes and the usual beech and oak. The trees are all suitably huge, befitting a place with royal connections.

In many hunting lodges the earthworks are more visible on the map than on the ground, but here they are prominent. The grassy paths that cross the area muffle the sound of footsteps and make the site feel reverential.

South-west of the Churchyard is a great mad oak (GR SU 208124). Its twisting trunk and monstrous branches stand out in an area of outstanding trees – resist climbing it if you can.

07 Anses Wood

GR SU 229124

A visit to Anses Wood is a pleasant experience. The bird life here is very varied, with tits predominating but woodpeckers often in attendance as well.

The name of the wood provides a puzzle with possible links to French, Nordic and Celtic. You can choose whether bay, handle, an arc segment (all French), to consider/think (Nordic) or troublesome (Celtic) fit this area of woodland.

If you are walking into the wood from the car park at Cadman's Pool you might notice that the track is built up into quite a high embankment. There are also some large flat bays beside the track. These features are all leftovers from a wartime bomb storage point. It was considered rather troublesome to store and handle bombs too close to the populated areas of the airfield so this out-of-the-way area was used.

The original tracks are the ones surrounding the 'P' on the OS map, along with the arc segment and track heading towards the entrance to South Bentley Inclosure. Whilst strolling along the track, perhaps pondering the name, it is worth considering that just north of here is Freeworms Hill. Trying to decipher the meaning of this name could really open up a can of worms . . .

08 Airfield clues tour

GR SU 248125

Stoney Cross Airfield covered an area of around 5km^2 spread over squares O7, O8, N7 and N8. There are several car parks in the vicinity from which to start a circular walk in search of clues from the 1940s. The 'airfield clues tour' includes a scoring system, based on different service ranks and airfield locations (see below), which you can take seriously or not. If you have parked in the car park opposite Long Beech campsite you are already following in 'Ike's' footsteps and have earned 1 point.

Rank:

- 1 point: Storeman
- 10 points: Ground crew
- 35 points: Flying officer
- 60 points: Group captain
- 100 points: Future President of the United States of America

Location (multiple points for multiple sightings (e.g. five open hard standings earns 5 points):

- Aircraft/car parking area visited by General 'Ike' Eisenhower: 1 point
- Assorted bricks or concrete connected with former buildings: 1 point
- Open hard standing: 1 point
- Forested hard standing: 2 points
- Floor of a former building: 5 points
- Runway light blocks (circular hole surrounded by concrete): 5 points (max. 20 pts)
- Remains of hard standings near Ocknell Pond: 5 points (max. 10 pts)
- Taxiway near Janesmoor Pond, Cadman's Pool or Stoney Cross Plain: 5 points (max. 15 pts)
- The intersection of any two of the three runways: 10 points (max. 30 pts)
- Site of the former water tank that older visitors will remember: 20 points

09 Rufus Stone

GR SU 270124

The inscription on the 'Rufus Stone' tells most of the story:

> *'Here stood an oak tree on which an arrow shot by Sir Walter Tyrell at a stag, glanced and struck King William the Second, surnamed Rufus, on the breast, of which he instantly died, on the second day of August, Anno 1100.*
>
> *King William the Second, surnamed Rufus being slain, as before related, was laid in a cart, belonging to one Purkis, and drawn from hence, to Winchester, and buried in the cathedral church of that city.*
>
> *That the spot where an event so memorable might not hereafter be forgotten; the enclosed stone was set up by John Lord Delaware who had seen the tree growing in this place.*
>
> *This stone having been much mutilated, and the inscriptions on each of its three sides defaced this more durable memorial with the original inscriptions was erected in the year 1841 by WM Sturges Bourne. Warden.'*

This modern cast-iron pillar sits under a younger oak tree than in the original story. What really happened on that day in August will never be truly known. Was it an accident or murder? Did Sir Walter Tyrell kill King William II by purposely glancing an arrow off a tree (or a stag, or boar)? Or was that story a falsehood or an exaggeration? What is known is that Rufus died and Sir Walter Tyrell immediately fled to Normandy. Such questions can be mulled over in the nearby Sir Walter Tyrell pub.

O10 Boundary Post

GR SU 283137

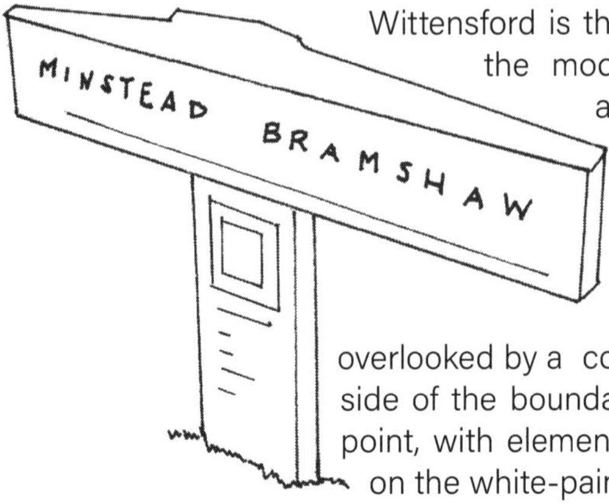

Wittensford is the site of the boundary between the modern-day parishes of Minstead and Bramshaw. For a short distance the boundary follows the unnamed stream formed by three 'gutters' – Shepherd's, King's Garn and Coalmeer. The ford is now a modern bridge overlooked by a couple of houses on the Bramshaw side of the boundary. It's a slovenly stream at this point, with elements of brown that match the rust on the white-painted boundary post.

Minstead is the real attraction here as most of the land in Bramshaw is farmland with limited access. South of the boundary there is a large area of woodland, starting with Little Eye Green and then Bignell Wood. There is also access under the A31 to Shave Green Inclosure. Little Eye Green is a very nice area of ancient woodland. Large oak and beech trees dominate but closer to the ground you'll see many moss lawns as well as the usual ferns and holly.

Among the variety of mosses found here, encouraged by the damp conditions around the ponds in the woodland, is sphagnum or 'peat' moss. Sphagnum moss has traditionally had many uses. It absorbs liquid astonishingly well and has been used as a wound dressing throughout history, including during the First World War. Bear Grylls fans can try to squeeze water from the moss (not recommended but if you are dying of thirst it is better than the alternative).

*Sometime during 2020 the boundary post was destroyed by a falling tree. The bridge railings have been repaired but the post is a shadow of its former self. You can use the illustration to help you see what it would have looked like!

O11 Shave Green Inclosure

GR SU 294130

For hundreds of years Cadnam has been an important transit point between Ringwood, Southampton, Romsey and Lyndhurst. Many roads come in and out of Cadnam but arguably none are as grand as the Douglas-fir-lined avenue through Shave Green Inclosure.

In 1945 E.W. Jones of the Imperial Forestry Institute, Oxford, wrote,

> *'. . . Shave Green, another Inclosure of the same period, where ride-side lines of Douglas make a splendid avenue through crops of oak, Scots pine and larch.'*
>
> (https://www.jstor.org/stable/pdfplus/2256558)

Douglas fir was first introduced to the UK in 1827 and the period spoken of is 1851–64. His 'splendid avenue' was then less than 100 years old; but it is now around 160 years old and even more splendid.

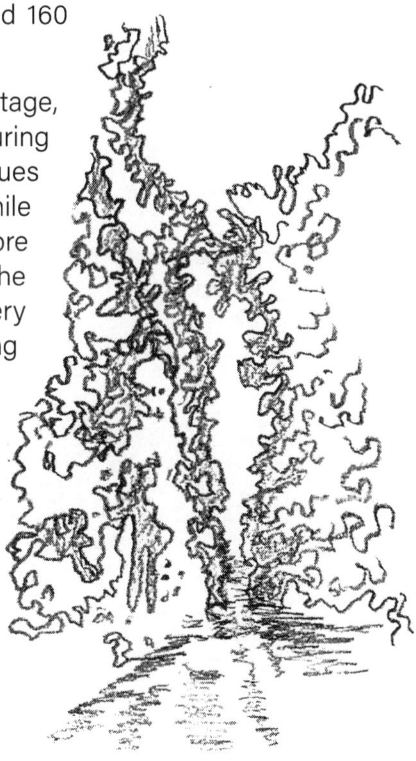

The avenue starts at Shave Green Cottage, built at the turn of the 20th century during the reign of Edward VII. It then continues in a straight line for almost exactly a mile in the direction of Malwood Castle before turning south and then fizzling out. The firs line most of the avenue and are very impressive at a number of spots, including the western end of the track where the path narrows.

Superb circular walks can be had from car parks at Clay I lill, Yolsham Hill, the Cricket Field, either of the village pubs in Cadnam or even the Rufus Stone car park. If you try this, as ever, be prepared for some navigation and some boggy patches!

O12 A tale of two village halls

GR SU 307138, 314123

The neighbouring villages of Copythorne and Bartley have village halls with very different styles. You could visit both or pick the one that sounds nicest. There's a pub halfway between them and a shop in case you wanted to picnic in the park at Copythorne.

This village of a hundred or so houses has a park, benches, a small playground and a village hall with a lot of chutzpah. It resembles many things depending on your vantage point (and viewpoint). It has been described as the bow of a boat (in homage to larger neighbour Southampton perhaps?) If sci-fi is your thing it might remind you of Star Wars or even Buck Rogers. Is it an avant-garde thank-you to an Admiral, General or Group Captain? Or is it a bat? And why is there a door halfway up a wall with a stylish metal ladder? 'KEEP OFF LADDER' says the sign, below the CCTV camera which would catch any miscreants.

Down the road Bartley Village Hall rejects grandiose, futuristic pretentions. It favours corrugated metal panels over concrete and brick; instead of 'massive', it is village-sized. Its little clock tower says 'middle England' and the eaves and doors are scrupulously white. This village hall is a lovingly looked-after tin hut of the sort you might find weathered and weather-beaten in the Falklands or Shetland. Its one eccentricity is perhaps its immense greenness. It is really green. Not quite royal green or British racing green, also not bottle green. Martian green perhaps?

O13 Netley Marsh metalwork

GR SU 332130

Netley Marsh is a small ribbon village overshadowed by its much larger neighbour, Totton. Though it lacks the charm of many New Forest villages it does boast a small school, a decent pub and St Matthew's Church.

If you are visiting towards the end of July the village is transformed by the Netley Marsh Steam & Craft Show. Operating since 1971, the show is a mecca for steam, bus, car and motorcycle enthusiasts. Music and fairground rides jostle for attention with more traditional forest activities such as horse riding and falconry.

Except at show time Netley Marsh is a sedate place. The focal points of the village are the pub and church and its first interesting feature lies between the two. Beside the bus stop is a grand metal bench suitable for at least four strangers and half a dozen or more prepared to relinquish their personal space. The rear of the bench is adorned with a crown, perhaps proclaiming this to be the Queen of Benches; no explanation is offered.

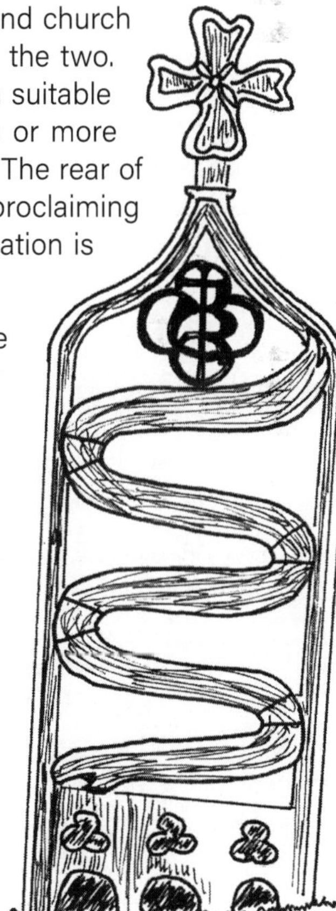

Within St Matthew's Churchyard are three metal grave markers, none with any wording left. Two are relatively ordinary; the third is ornate yet amazingly simple. It is decorated with two crosses and two apparent references to serpents. It is a very unusual sight in an otherwise quite ordinary graveyard.

P3 Frankenbury

GR SU 166151

Frankenbury is a place to visit if you are a fan of Iron Age forts. With dimensions of 300 x 300 metres Frankenbury looks very imposing on the map. The reality is more elusive, as you might expect from something over 2000 years old. The southern and western flanks make use of a natural promontory and would provide a great lookout over the River Avon if weren't for the trees. To the north and east the earthworks are less obvious due to age and wear.

Frankenbury is also a place to visit if you enjoy a walk in the woods. The woodland that has grown up around the site is well looked after, with a fine selection of broadleaved and coniferous trees. The nature trail from the amusingly named Sandy Balls Holiday Park passes through here and is worth following.

Finally, Frankenbury is a place to come if you want to sit back and imagine. What would life have been like for an Iron Age warrior keeping watch over the ramparts? Did Roman centurions camp here, or perhaps Ecgberht, King of Wessex?

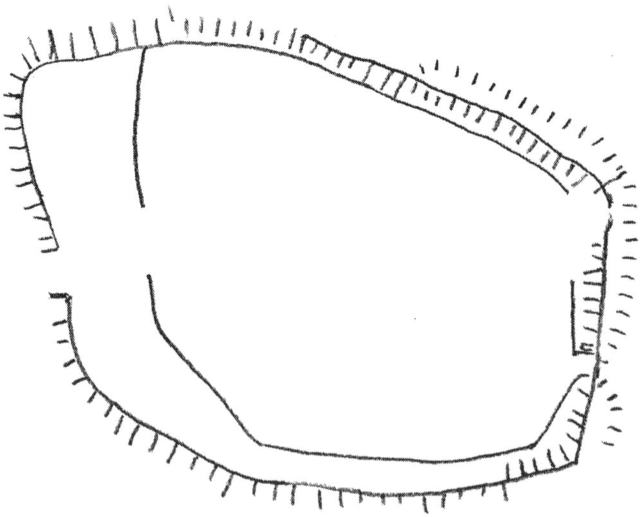

P4 Gorse

GR SU 182150

Rob Hayward, son of John Hayward, author of *Dartmoor 365*, has kindly given me permission to reproduce square J2 from that outstanding book. I have quoted the text exactly as it was written as it applies to Godshill as well as at least another 100 squares in the New Forest.

'When gorse is in blossom
Kissing's in fashion'. . .

. . . which means, as everyone knows, that there is never a day when a kiss would be out of season. This is not because gorse (or furze or whin) is such a remarkable plant that it blooms throughout the year, but because there are two species which have different flowering periods. The taller European (or common) gorse blooms from roughly December to June, while western gorse, a lower, more compact shrub, is normally in flower from July to November. The species can therefore be identified by consulting a calendar, or perhaps your watch. Here beside the road both kinds are to be found. In some seasons there might be a slight overlap so occasionally it is possible to find at least a few of each species at the same time. The stature of the bush and the number of new buds or dead flowers will usually sort them out. If not then examine the tiny bract at the base of any flower. If it is at least 2mm wide and also wider than the flower stalk then the species will be European gorse.

Difficult as it is to handle, gorse has been an extremely useful plant to country folk. As fodder for horses or cattle it is very nutritious, though of course it has to be well pounded first. This could be done with a mallet or in an apple crusher. It was even sown as a crop for this purpose.

Gorse burns well even when green, and it was once a popular fuel for bread ovens. The ashes contain a good deal of alkali, and can be used as a substitute for soap. Then there was wine and a yellow dye to be made from the flowers, and walking sticks from the stems.

If you are passing a gorse bush in late summer and hear clicks and snaps you are listening to the ripe seed pods splitting open.

In August grayling butterflies are to be found on this common. They are not easy to spot where they rest in the grass with retracted and camouflaged wings.' (Hayward, 1991, p163)

P5 Ashley Walk Bombing Range

GR SU 208143, 200141, 199141

There are three key features in this square – all well worth visiting.

Firstly, looking every bit like a perfectly evil Lego building staring with three squinting eyes out over the heath, stands a Second World War observation shelter. The view from the shelter totally misses the site of the real action (more of this later). There is a very useful overview and map of the area in the shelter. From this you can see that the observation shelter overlooked the Fragmentation Targets in square P6.

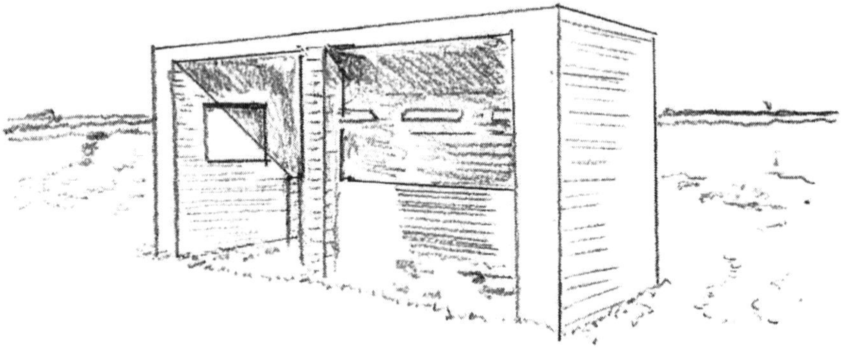

The Orwellian-sounding Ministry of Home Security Target is marked on the map as a large tumulus. Under the mound is a large concrete structure, used to test the impact of bombs. Although it was often referred to as a submarine pen its construction was a lot less robust than the German submarine pens in northern France. After the war it was considered simpler to bury the structure rather than try to remove it.

The 'pond' 100 metres south west of the 'pen' is the result of the largest bomb ever dropped on the UK. A Grand Slam bomb, or Ten Ton Tess as it was affectionately known due to its weight, was tested here on 13th March 1945. The resulting crater was impressive enough for the bombs to be deployed on targets such as coastal batteries, bridges and actual submarine pens. On a peaceful New Forest day it is hard to imagine an earthquake bomb being dropped just metres from where you stand.

P6 Coopers Hill Holes and targets

GR SU 209148

Coopers Hill has a number of round features on an otherwise flat plain. Rather like a miniature version of the large frying pan in square Q5, a smaller chalk version sits at GR SU 209148. This is an aiming marker between Fragmentation Targets C & D and the highlight of this square. The aiming marker helped aircrew to release their bombs at the precise moment they needed to. The Fragmentation Targets were used to help test the relative vulnerabilities of different types of aircraft blast pens to fragmentation bombs. The chalk has prevented the heather and gorse from obscuring the circular shape and it is quite easy to spot from the track, just north of the Crock Hill junction.

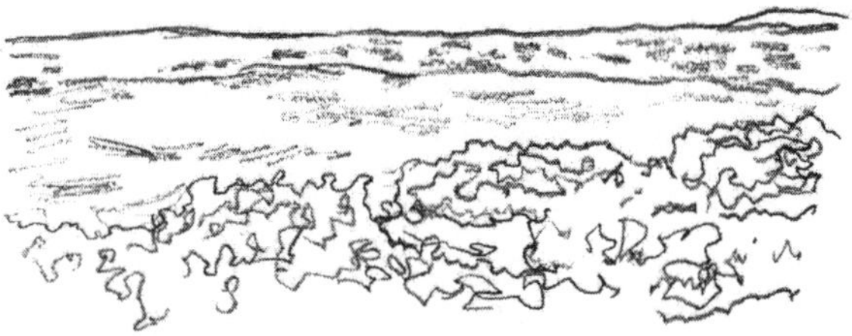

North of the aiming marker, on the way to The Butts, are several bomb craters and the target indicator for Fragmentation Target D. The craters are sometimes tricky to spot and you often need to be on top of them to notice them. Most of the craters across the whole bombing range were filled in after the war. If you are able to count 10 in this area you have been very successful, though the square pond at The Butts would be a dubious inclusion in your total. Fragmentation Target D has sprouted a couple of trees, in defiance of the chalk.

Two hundred metres south-southwest of the aiming marker is Fragmentation Target C. All that remains is a small semicircle of chalk. Further exploration would reveal more craters, though they look similar to the ones you have already seen.

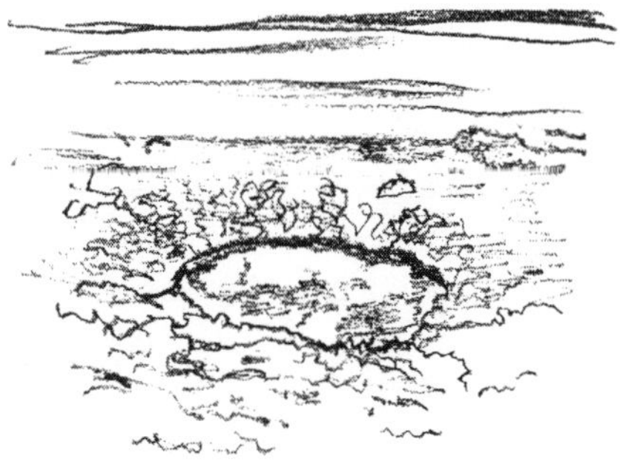

P7 The Royal Oak

GR SU 232141

If the weather is good, the beer garden at the Royal Oak in Fritham is without parallel.

It's a small pub, 'wonderfully compact' in their words, and sharing tables inside is encouraged, if not required. However, when the sun is high in the sky, it is the beer garden that fills with customers. The size of a small field, it has picnic benches and blanket-sized areas of grass all around. There are plenty of places to park bikes or horses and dogs; children and Duke of Edinburgh Award participants are all equally welcome. At busy times there is a serving hatch on the side of the pub meaning you don't need to leave the sun-dappled lawn to get your food and drink.

Dating from the 1600s, the cosy pub is part thatched, part brick and part mock-Tudor. It's a building with a lot of history, and is part of New Forest folklore these days. The pictures dotted around the bar record New Forest people and pastimes through the years.

If you are keen on locally-produced food, this is a Royal Oak speciality. Indeed, the cattle in the field and the pigs in the surrounding woods are all destined for the menu once they've had their fill of grass/acorns.

P8 Longcross Plain

GR SU 244151

Longcross Plain is not the highest point in the New Forest (just) but has the highest trig point (just). Other than roads there are not too many features on this plain plain. The two highlights are the pond and the nearby trig point.

The 'roof' of the New Forest above the 125-metre contour is very flat and concentrated in the area north of Fritham. The trig point at this location is on the 125m contour line but it is hard to judge where the true high point is; wherever you stand another point close by seems just a little higher. When you walk there and look back, the place you were now appears higher. The OS team might have had the same issue and decided that the highest point on the plain was the one closest to the road.

Just 300 metres away is Longcross Pond. Slightly below the trig point and bending the contour around it, the pond is a popular place for ponies. This is the site of another optical illusion: the pond and the trig point are barely perceptible when each is viewed from the other. Bright weather is needed to view the trig point, as any greyness causes it to blend in with the trees in the background. A full pond is also needed as a lack of water prevents any reflection and the bank is hard to spot. Shorter people are at a distinct disadvantage here, though standing on the trig point would doubtless alleviate the issue.

P9 Broken (Brook) Wood tree graveyard

GR SU 264143

The epicentre of this large area of fallen trees appears to be an ancient beech with huge conjoined limbs, its crevassed, moss-coated trunk sheltering fungi and its knobbly roots erupting all around.

Around the ancient beech the carcasses of huge oak and beech trees litter the landscape. The fallen trees show the immense power of wind and gravity. The prone trunks of the largest trees are intact but spread out their branches are spread out like fans. Some shattered trees are still standing, wounded limbs hanging from their trunks. This scene continues up Brook Hill, but throughout the wood hundreds more healthy trees still stand proud.

The New Forest is a place of enchantment and folklore; so was this carnage the handiwork of the 'boot' of Broom Hill, kicking away at branches and trees? Although shown on the map it exists only in your imagination on the ground as every dip and rise appears to mark a boundary. It's not until you reach Ravens Nest Inclosure or Fountain Court that you are reminded what a boundary actually looks like. Is the boot a cartographic error, an experiment in symbology or a hint of other forces at work?

Gangs of fleet-footed deer tear around these woods but it seems unlikely they are to blame for the demise of such massive trees. In an area with place-names including broom, raven and gibbet perhaps suspicion should fall upon the witches of Burley. More mundanely the relative height of the area, exposing these ancient trees to extreme weather, might be the answer.

P10 Brook

GR SU 273140

Brook is a small and dispersed hamlet surrounded in all directions by a combination of farmland and woodland. A small brook, Shepherd's Gutter, has a confluence in the village, hence its name. This larger stream leads down to Cadnam and then takes its name from that village.

When standing on the pedestrian bridge over the brook you would be remiss not to notice the wonderful thatched buildings all around.

There are two cottages, both with drooping thatched eaves. Other than the thatch, the cottages are quite different in style and both have a wonderful variety of different trees in the gardens. As you discuss the merits of each cottage and the pros and cons of thatched gate archways, do not forget to turn around.

The Green Dragon pub is a more formal thatched building. In the spring and summer it also has a stunning display of flowers in hanging baskets and wall baskets, on windowsills and atop the portico. Dating from the 18th century, it would be worthy of any hamlet. Brook is no ordinary hamlet though, and has a second pub on the opposite side of the road. The Bell Inn is better suited to those who shun cute thatched buildings. An imposing, tiled-roofed building, it allows you to have a pub crawl in a hamlet and stay over in the hotel should you wish.

P11 Cadnam Green donkey common

GR SU 294143

Cadnam Green, not to be confused with the larger Cadnam Common to the north, is a sliver of common land, unusual both in its shape and the fact that it has not been incorporated into the surrounding fields. Stretching around 500m from north to south it is only 125m at its widest with a smaller section beside the road a little further to the north.

The chief features here are the two ponds and some impressive trees marking the edge of the common land. The ponds attract horses, ponies and donkeys to the area, much to the annoyance of the occasional motorists. During wet periods the surrounding grassed areas become very boggy and water drains down to the nearby tributary of the Cadnam River. A footpath leads east, then south from Cadnam Green to join the river and shares an unusual tunnel under the M27.

Due to the proximity of the motorway and the dampness of the ground this is not a place to linger. That is, of course, unless you are equine, whereby you have food, water and a tin-roofed shelter in case of inclement weather.

P12 The Compass Inn

GR SU 318143

This is a pub with a number of superlatives connected to it. The Compass Inn claims, with some justification, to be the most dog-friendly pub in the New Forest. All dogs are welcomed by the management, provided they are accompanied by well-behaved owners. All food is gluten-free with a very informative menu for those with any dietary needs or wishes.

The building itself has a Tardis-like quality: the pub seems very small from the outside. It has a decent-sized beer garden, and is surely the only pub in the New Forest with its own charity shop.

Aptly, there is a superb example of a nautical compass mounted in the bar. Whether you have travelled south from Copythorne Common cricket ground, west from Tatchbury Mount, north from Ringwood Road or east from Copythorne Church, you'll find the bar staff directly south of the compass.

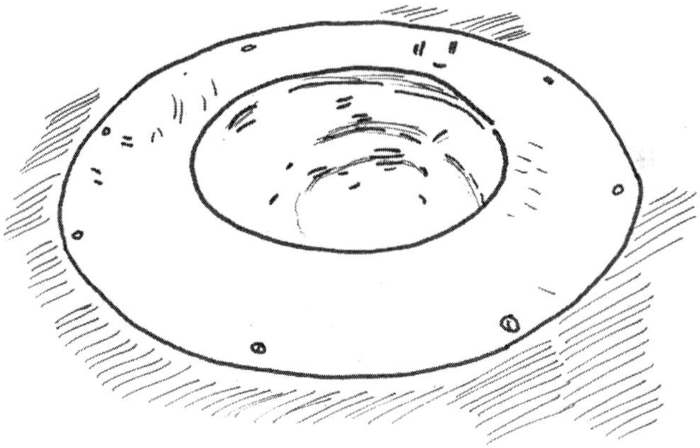

P13 A brutalist arch

GR SU 334140

Possibly the most interesting, and certainly the ugliest, entrance to the New Forest, this is a product of the 2009 widening of the A326 and is marked as a subway on the map. And what a subway it is! At approximately 10m wide, 10m high and 50m long you could hide a missile launcher in here. The brutalist concrete structure would certainly be more at home in North Korea than marking the boundary of a national park.

Nature is doing its best to camouflage the dull grey concrete, which is approached from both sides by a narrow track. On the Totton side, housing has gradually filled in the gaps left by planners who most likely dreamt of slip roads, underpasses and free-flowing traffic rather than a muddy track.

The subway is best approached from Calmore, leaving a pleasant housing estate and travelling through a portal into the New Forest. Tatchbury Mount is very interesting in itself. Formerly an imposing gentleman's residence, it was sold to Hampshire County Council in 1927 so they could open a 'Colony for Mental Defectives'. A hospital still exists on the site though the grand old house is gone.

Q2 Many bridges

GR SU 154155

Although the River Avon has its source in Wiltshire and its mouth in Dorset it does spend part of its journey meandering through both Hampshire and the New Forest. Though it might seem to be a natural western border for the New Forest, making it so would have simply added a lot of high-value farmland with poor public access.

North east of Fordingbridge the River Avon forms the boundary of the New Forest and is then encompassed. In this area access through the farmland is interesting and access to the river quite easy. This spot is one of the best places in Hampshire to view the Avon. Although it lacks a picnic spot it does have a suspension bridge, built after the Second World War utilising parts from a military Bailey bridge. On the path to Folds Farm there are further bridges that look like they have military origins. This path across the flood plain is highly recommended, with its selection of steel bridges, brick bridges and concrete bridges. Count them if you wish; there are many.

Q3 Castle Hill

GR SU 170166

Castle Hill *Ring and Bailey* is written on the map, just south of the viewpoint on an extension of Castle Hill ridge. New Forest castles are not impressive in the way that stone-built castles, such as Barnard Castle in County Durham, are. You wouldn't catch people travelling long distances, under difficult circumstances, to visit this castle, even if there is a Specsavers in nearby Ringwood.

Due to the underwhelming nature of Castle Hill's 'castle' I initially planned to reproduce the lyrics to Ed Sheeran's 'Castle on the Hill' on this page. It's an upbeat, positive song that you could enjoy whilst looking at the small bailey covered in trees. Sadly, Ed's 'people' proved difficult to negotiate with so I've moved the focus of the square to the viewpoint.

The highlight here is the view: you can look across the roaring fields and River Avon into Dorset. Watching the sunset from Castle Hill is highly recommended as is bird watching if you are so inclined. This is possibly the steepest sustained slope in the New Forest, dropping from 60 to 35m above sea level.

The more adventurous may wish to clamber down through the trees to the banks of the Avon. This should not be undertaken lightly, as the slope is very steep and the ground slippery. The easiest place to attempt it is close to the Castle site. When you get to the bottom, hopefully without rolling, you'll find a lot of very damp ground – boots would be a wise choice.

Chestnut trees line the top of the ridge so from September to November is a good time to visit. It's a nice feeling to be on your way home, driving at forty down those country lanes, with a bag full of chestnuts to roast.

Q4 Bats

GR SU 177160

Far from being a creature to fear, bats are actually very vulnerable and in need of our protection. The New Forest provides a rich habitat for bats and between 13 and 16 of the 17 native species live in the area (recognition can be difficult, hence the difference in figures). Very rare bats such as the Bechstein's bat and barbastelle have made the Forest their home and all bat varieties are protected by law.

Bats tend to live in trees, often inhabiting holes left by woodpeckers or natural folds or twists in the timber. Old barns, tunnels and bridges are also favourites, especially during the winter, when bats hibernate.

Bats can be found across the New Forest, though proximity to trees and insects are key. Dusk during summer and autumn are the best times to spot bats as they head out to feed. Bats can be identified by their jerky flight, which is due to their echolocation navigation system that quickly allows them to locate prey as well as obstructions. The bats flit from insect to insect, eating up to 1,000 an hour! For anyone who has been bugged by mosquitoes or midges the sight of bats comes as a blessed relief.

Godshill Inclosure is a good place to spot bats as there is an active campaign to increase colonies in the area. If you look high up in the trees you will notice bat boxes, built to provide protection. Sadly neither nearby Frankenbury or Castle Hill provides ruined gothic ramparts for the bats to roost in.

Q5 The Giant Frying Pan

GR SU 205156

Ashley Walk Bombing Range once covered several square miles but the most obvious sign of it on the OS map is here. On the map there is something resembling a 200-metre-wide frying pan with a short, stubby handle. It is clearly man-made as the 'pan' is perfectly circular and there are tracks leading to and from it.

On the ground there is also something that is clearly man-made. The 'pan' is a large and totally flat sand and chalk apron. The ground is completely bare for the most part though nature is beginning to encroach in places.

This area was the site of No. 2 Wall Target in the 1940s, offering bombers a long reinforced wall to practise dropping a variety of ordnance. In fact most bombing runs were at low level and the bombs were launched into the face of the wall. If that seems an odd idea, just think about Barnes Wallis' bouncing bombs and picture the walls as dams in the Ruhr valley. No. 1 Wall Target was close to Little Cockley Plain and No. 3 Wall Target was near Bur Bushes.

Although the walls no longer exist this area is great for exploration. There are numerous chalk markers which vegetation is struggling to reclaim. Live bomb testing across the range resulted in countless small ponds, for which the ponies are always grateful.

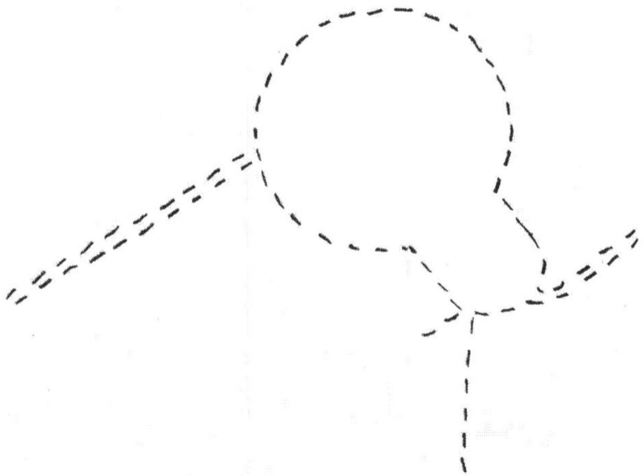

Q6 The reflection pond

GR SU 210156

The initial challenge with this pond is to find it. If you are walking along the flat part of The Butts on Ashley Walk and you find a pond then you've found the wrong one. A lot of the ponds here are a result of practice bombing when this area was known as Ashley Ranges – this one, maybe not.

To find the pond you need to find the small re-entrant (a U-shape in the contour lines) directly north west of the path junction at the 111 spot height on the OS map. As you drop into the re-entrant the ground becomes marshier. The pond is on the northern side of the boggy ground. If it has been raining this area is likely to be very wet. Even in very dry conditions the pond seems to remain full.

It is a small pond, around five metres in circumference, but with crystal clear water around half a metre deep. You probably will not notice it until you are within a few metres. The bottom has lots of flints which are very common around here together with a clay that keeps the water where it is.

What you do when you find the pond is up to you. You should probably pat yourself on the back if you found it easily. Photographers will want to set their cameras up in order to take any manner of cool shots. Using the pool to contemplate and reflect on life is another good use.

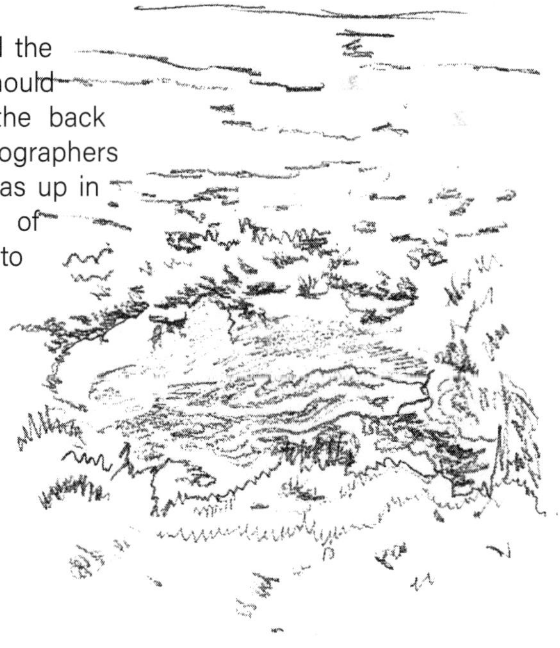

Q7 Bramshaw Telegraph

GR SU 228167

Bramshaw Telegraph not only is one of the highest spots in the New Forest, it also feels like it. A south-westerly weather system rolling in is clearly visible and the rain comes as a disappointment, but not a surprise. A few buildings cluster on the edge of the forest but they offer no clues to the telegraph aspect of the name.

It is the height and the view that are the reasons for the name, though it is now over 200 years out of date. In 1795, during the French Revolutionary Wars, the Admiralty decided to build a series of telegraph stations between south-coast ports and London to warn of any French invasion. A system of six optical shutter signals sent coded messages at speed. Bramshaw, on the route from Plymouth, proved an ideal spot to set up a telegraph station.

The Battle of Waterloo and the defeat of Napoleon signalled the demise of the telegraph. The wooden towers were dismantled and all signs of the Bramshaw Telegraph disappeared, with the exception of the name. However, the fantastic view remains and on a clear day it is interesting to work out just how far you can see; hopefully, more than just approaching storm clouds.

Q8 Pipers Wait

GR SU 249166

Pipers Wait is the highest point in the New Forest, undisputed except by those people who still believe it is Telegraph Hill, 2km to the west. To be on the safe side, for those who are 'peak-baggers', a 'ridge walk' can be undertaken. From Pipers Wait this would cross Black Bush Plain to the trig point (125m) on Longcross Plain. A slight dip then takes you up Homy Ridge (125m+), Telegraph Hill (125m+) and onto the trig point (124m) just south of Pound Bottom. On this 5km route you will have undulated barely 50m and seen a lot of heathland.

Finding the top at Pipers Wait itself is difficult. The car park itself is often regarded as the top but land all around it appears just a little bit higher. One contender is the covered reservoir at GR SU 246165, just south of the highest house in the New Forest. Unmentioned on the map, unlabelled on the ground and straddling the Hampshire-Wiltshire border, this reservoir does a good impression of being a rabbit warren. The giveaway is the extraordinary number and variety of manhole covers in the vicinity. It is almost impossible for a group of people to count them all and agree on the number.

Perhaps a covered reservoir is too man-made to count as the top anyway. What is for sure is that as you wander around searching for the highest point you are surrounded by wonderful woodland. Both Crow's Nest Bottom and Two Beeches Bottom are worth an exploration, as well as offering an opportunity to count beeches and crow's nests.

Q9 The gonzo church of St Peter's, Bramshaw

GR SU 265166

A church in a jumble of styles. Slate roof, tiled buttress, plastered brick, a solid brick tower adorned with an American-style belfry, mixed brick and flint in the style of Tetris gone wrong, layered brick and stone, pure stone, even buttresses side by side in different styles. The next two buttresses different to each other in a different way. Is the ivy holding it all together? A little half-brick, half-wood lean-to toilet with a roof made of one-third clear plastic and two-thirds slate, stairs up to a white door set in a fully plastered wall, another lean-to (cement?) Taller and with a black gutter, the next white door has no step but a ramp and a porch roofed with bitumen sheet. White window, black window, brick courses don't match, pineapple chimney, odd cross and weather vane. Door gone, all the buildings intersect, this time windows match! Time you sat down under the yew ....

St Peter's Church is such a mix of styles that I have used the Gonzo style of writing coined by the late Hunter S. Thompson to describe it. Bizarre and idiosyncratic are words used to describe Gonzo journalism, and they can be equally applied to the church.

Q10 Furzley crossroads

GR SU 286163

This unassuming little crossroads has much of mild interest within a short distance. The crossroads has a signpost indicating the distances to eight places, two in each direction. The furthest place is Wellow, at 2¾ miles; the closest Penn Common, just ½ mile away. The first point of interest is that 6 of the 8 places mentioned on the sign have fractions of distance (e.g. Nomansland is 1¾ miles away). Are there any signposts in the New Forest with more fractions?

On ¾ of the sides of the crossroads there are points of interest. To the west is a small post box on a pole. To the east is a former phone box that has been converted into a library. Feel free to borrow a book, or even drop one off. If you find a good book a delightful place to sit and read on a sunny day is just 300m south of the road junction. Stagbury Hill is a Bronze Age burial mound converted into a rabbit warren in the Middle Ages and finally into a trigonometry point in recent times.

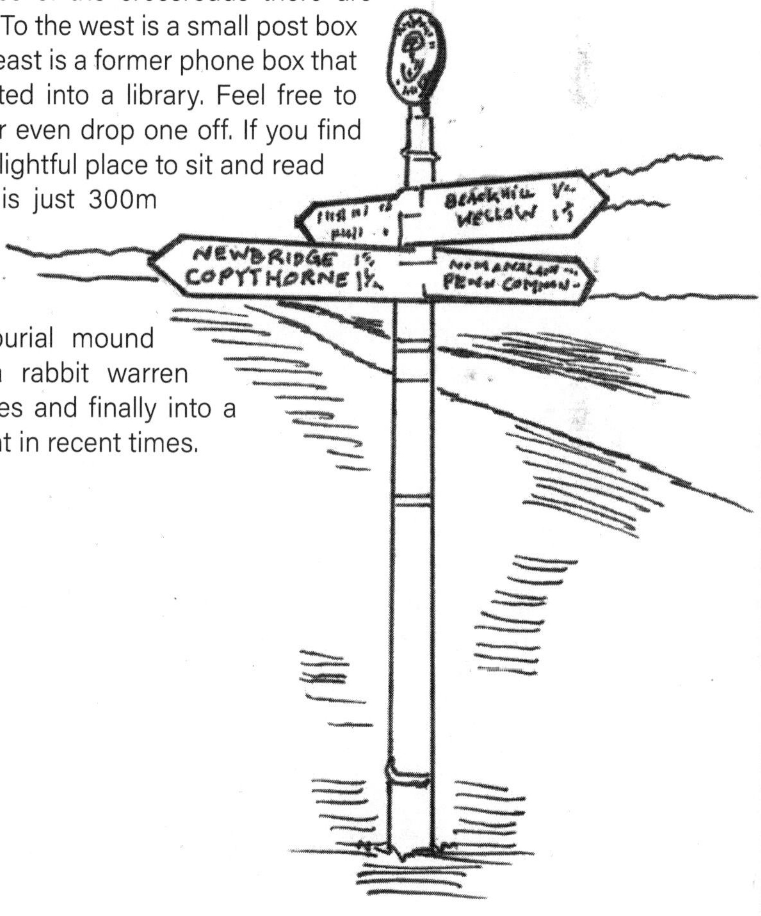

Q11 Rabbit warrens

GR SU 293169

Half Moon Common, along with neighbouring Furzley Common, contains several medieval rabbit warrens. These were hills, natural mounds, or in some cases burial mounds, that were used to farm rabbits or hares. In many cases additional banks and barriers were built to contain the rabbits, or at least make them easier to catch. A warrener would often live just next to the site to protect it from poachers, foxes, dogs, etc. The rabbits provided meat and fur as well as a good source of income for the warrener. Warrens such as these were common from the 12th century and in some cases survived until the 1950s when myxomatosis decimated rabbit populations across the UK.

Other than Stagbury Hill (Q10) the best examples are Half Moon Hill, which has a large and small mound, and just to the south of this, Warren Hill. Warren Hill is shown as an area of private land but is fully accessible. Just north of Duck Hill is a hexagonal dyke system of a similar shape to the warrens. Whether this is a further example I do not know, just as I am not sure how Duck Hill got its name. However, a clue to Duck Hill's name is the number of small streams on the common. It probably would not be a duck's first choice of home, but it would not be too bad, especially if the friendly locals provided food.

Q12 'Dark Hedges' - *Game of Thrones* comes to the New Forest

GR SU 325170

This corner of the New Forest is affected by its proximity to Totton, Southampton and the transport links to Salisbury and beyond. The boundary of the park is the A36 and as a result it can feel very busy. However, tucked behind a pub and motel is a short but interesting stretch of road.

Those who have not seen *Game of Thrones* may not know Bregagh Road near Armoy, Northern Ireland. The 'Kingsroad', known as Dark Hedges, is a tunnel of ancient beech trees used as a scene in the series and now a major tourist attraction. The road has now been closed to most vehicles as the area has become increasingly popular.

The New Forest's own Kingsroad is not as dramatic or as mature as the 200-year-old trees in Northern Ireland. These oaks have their own style and intent though, with branches interlinking over the road. With time this tunnel of trees will only improve and in another hundred years tourists may well be flooding to this area.

Currently the main beneficiaries of the view are the golfers heading to Paultons Golf Centre. A walk or drive to the clubhouse (Q12) reveals some well-tended mixed woodland, many in rows sectioning off holes. Beside the lake on Allmoor Copse is a memorial plaque which reads: 'Planted in loving memory of Peter Makepeace, 1933–2005. His dying wish was to join his balls in the lake. His favourite hole.'

Another link to *Game of Thrones* are the blood-curdling screams that can be frequently heard. In the TV series death and destruction are rife; in the New Forest the cause is the white-knuckle rides of Paulton's Family Theme Park. Fear not.

R3 Woodgreen Village Hall murals

GR SU 171176

Woodgreen is an attractive little village of just over 500 people on the edge of the New Forest. It has a pub and a community-run shop, but its most amazing feature lies tucked away in the village hall.

When a new village hall was being built in 1930–31, two students from the Royal College of Art were commissioned to paint murals of village life inside the hall. They were paid for their work by the Carnegie Trust, an organisation set up by Scottish-American Andrew Carnegie, a well-known philanthropist and one of the richest Americans of all time.

The artists, Robert Baker and Edward Payne, spent 18 months painting rural scenes, taking villagers as their subjects. The results were stunning. The murals cover the entire interior of the main hall and deal with all aspects of village life, including a visit to Castle Hill (Q3). The villagers are named, but only a few are still alive. If you look at the 'health and safety' in some of the pictures it is a wonder anyone survived to adulthood. In a possible departure from their brief, above a doorway the artists painted a rather spooky scene with a full moon, bats, an owl and a scarecrow with a pumpkin head.

If the hall is not open, you can peek through the window for a partial view. Alternatively, the murals can be seen at www.woodgreenvillagehall.org.uk/home/murals/slideshow. A mosaic, again inspired by village life, was commissioned for the millennium and sits above the entrance to the hall.

R4 Hale Park Avenue

GR SU 183187

Although Hale House and Park is not open to the public, part of the wonderful lime-tree avenue is. The Avon Valley Path passes Hale House on the route between the lovely towns of Fordingbridge and Downton. A footpath along the dismantled railway line can make this a circular walk; though there is a kilometre of unpleasant walking along Salisbury Road on the Hants/Wilts border.

The lime tree avenue flanks the drive leading from the gatehouse, across Hale Park, to the front door of the house. Mistletoe and crows have moved into the higher branches and loud rattle-like chatter fills the air. In the spring daffodils add to the colour. To the side are beech trees, including one tree cleaved in two, providing fine action-photo opportunities for those who like staging karate chops or clambering through trees.

The house itself dates from 1715 and can be resplendent in red or green vegetation in the correct season. Huge columns dominate the front of the house and are a marked contrast to the tinny clock that marks the hour. The house and grounds were designed, built and owned by Thomas Archer, an important character in Queen Anne's court. One of his official roles as Groom Porter was to: 'adjudicate in disputes which arose in gaming at Court'.

R5 Hale Purlieu

GR SU 197185

A purlieu, under Forest Law, is an area that used to be part of a Royal Forest but is now regarded as an outlying area. Hale Purlieu ceased to be part of the New Forest in 1280 and did not return until 1964. It is now owned by the National Trust, who have kept man-made objects, including bridges, to a minimum, so wellingtons are recommended. There is a free car park in the south-west corner.

Almost 700 years outside the Forest boundary has not done the area any harm (power lines excepted) and it is an important area for birds, butterflies and all manner of bog flora.

Birch and oak on the shoulders of the valley soon give way to bracken, heather, gorse and then bog. Dotted around are numerous apple trees which, along with the red berries of the rowan trees, are immensely popular with the birds.

Colour is everywhere during the autumn as the oak and birch turn yellow and the ferns traffic-light from green to amber and finally dead brown. Whites and creams of mushrooms can be mistaken for the flint that makes up a large part of the soil here. Heather flowers purple and white whilst blackberries wait to be eaten. Occasional flicks of yellow indicate new-growth gorse and in some of the rowans green mistletoe berries hide amongst the red. If the weather has been wet you'll also see white clouds reflected in the puddles.

R6 The Secret Forest

GR SU 224179

This grid reference lies approximately in the middle of the 'secret forest'. To the north the forest includes Pimlico Firs and Bottom. To the south Franchises Common and Wood are included, along with Burnt Ground Wood.

The name 'secret forest' comes from the fact that until recently the wood had been in private ownership for hundreds of years. Access has been restricted to a couple of paths and the natural treasures were pretty much unknown. Rare lichen had attracted an SSSI designation to some parts of the woodland and management had been sympathetic outside the commercially-logged areas.

In 2018 the RSPB took over almost 1,000 acres of woodland here and renamed it Franchises Lodge Nature Reserve. Some of the land was in lieu of a large tax bill, and the purchase of the rest was funded by the National Park, Friends of the New Forest and a large legacy to the RSPB. This was a fine example of organisations and individuals working together for the greater good!

At the time of publishing the RSPB is still slowly investigating the flora and fauna it has taken over. Increased public access to the land is in the process of being organised, with RSPB signs appearing around the forest. Organised tours are available and are a great way to spot the firecrest, wood warbler and goshawk that are known to frequent the woods.

R7 The Pentagon

GR SU 230186

One for the cartographers and conspiracy theorists. Viewed on an OS map this area is heavily wooded but includes a ½km^2 clearing with a shape that has more than a passing resemblance to Australia. Google Maps also shows this general area to be heavily wooded. However, within the clearing is a clear silver-grey pentagon. There's already enough material for conspiracy theorists to conclude that this is an alien landing area aligned with Uluru/Ayer's Rock in Australia.

The truth is more prosaic. As you walk towards the site cows in pastures give way to rhododendron bushes, then to beech trees, then to pine, then gorse, briars, grass, ferns and much more besides till finally a solar array appears. It's a big solar array, the largest in the New Forest, but if you were cycling you would probably miss it. The public bridleway is the only place from which it is visible, unless you happen to be in a plane or perhaps a UFO. Hiding a solar farm this large is an impressive feat and is the only reason planning permission was granted.

This particular solar farm produces enough electricity to power around 1,500 homes, which would equate to all of the villages within five miles. The area under the panels has been returned to heathland which provides grazing for sheep. This is a great example of blending modern technology into an ancient forest with positive results.

R8 The Well of Sacrifice, Nomansland

GR SU 254173

This site is hard to locate on the OS map due to the poor placement of the large blue tankard indicating the pub opposite. What you actually find here is one of the most impressive war memorials in the New Forest. A small wood and brick edifice sits on a concrete plinth. Inside are the names of the fallen and those who served during both World Wars. Above the iron gates is the inscription 'The Well of Sacrifice' and a small wooden cross.

Oak trees stand guard beside it. There is obviously a well or spring underneath which supplied water to the pond next to it. During dry periods the pond is often emptied by thirsty animals.

Nomansland is an unusual name for an English village. It derives from its position on the border between Wiltshire and Hampshire and also right on the edge of the royal hunting grounds. In order to steer clear of the Forest Law's severe penalties it made sense to try and live outside anyone's jurisdiction. At certain points in history this was the role fulfilled by living in Nomansland.

R9 Landford Common

GR SU 258184

'Landford Common' is emblazoned across the map between New Road and Broomhill. A comparison with nearby Plaitford Common shows that only a very small rectangle of land is actually open-access: all the productive and/or dry land in this area has been turned into farmland or built upon. The small area left over is the land no one wanted – wet, acidic and boggy. As is so often the case though, this land is sometimes the most hospitable for wildlife, and Landford Bog is protected by many different organisations and run by the Wiltshire Wildlife Trust.

When you first enter the area it appears that silver birch reigns supreme. The soil here clearly suits them and some of the pathways take you through densely-woven woodland. Wherever the trees have died or are dying fungi thrive. The most common type is Birch Polymore. As the name suggests, it grows exclusively on birch trees. Known as a cure for many things, it was carried 5,300 years ago by Otzi, the Bronze Age man whose body was found in the Alps in 1991. The rule with this type of fungus is that if it looks like wood and feels like wood then it tastes like wood.

Beyond the woodland is the reason this area was never developed. The bog has two parts: the first is like heathland and the second is blanket bog. The second part is best admired from a distance, partly to conserve nature and partly to preserve your dry feet.

You need to look carefully to spot a lot of the nature. Flora includes bluebells, purple moor grass, hog asphodel, bogbean, marsh gentian and the carnivorous fly-eating sundew. Fauna includes raft spiders, frogs, tiger beetles and dragonflies. Many of these make very tasty meals for birds, adding to the attraction of Landford Bog for visitors with wings as well as wellingtons.

R10 Canada, West Wellow and Plaitford Common(s)

GR SU 279184

The map suggests that this square mile of tufty grassland separating several small villages is rather dull. However, investigation on the ground reveals it to be well worth a visit. Probably the best way to explore the Common(s) is to simply start walking and turn right (or left) each time you come to a boundary until you arrive back where you started. If you get too lost, head up a hill to try to spot where you came from.

The area to the north of West Wellow Common becomes very boggy and in wet weather the stream flowing under the A36 can flow at quite a rate. A lot of this water comes from springs along the eastern boundary of the Common. The western side has its own drainage basin centred on Sturtmoor Pond. Numerous bridges aid navigation here.

Though relatively flat, there is a trig point (45m) in the northeast corner of the Common, on a prominent hill (though not at the top of it, which is a metre higher). This is not the highest point of the Common, though; the centre of Plaitford Common has a more subtle hill which eventually peaks at 49 metres. In the dip between the two hills there is little sign of the roads and villages that surround you and it feels far more remote than it is.

The south of the Common has a Civil Parish Boundary with a prominent tumulus and mound to visit. Deazle Wood is also worth a quick visit if you are pining for the sight of trees.

R11 Canada

GR SU 289180

I'm going to describe Canada. Large, detached homesteads with good-sized gardens and room for a 4x4 or two. Rectangular plots of land, the shape of Saskatchewan or Manitoba. An expanse of land all around, sparsely populated except for the four-legged wildlife. Well-off, friendly locals who like to spend their time in the local chapels or the inn. Numerous silver birch trees giving way to grasslands as far as the eye can see. Approximately 3km from the grave of Florence Nightingale?

The Canada in the New Forest does match the description above, but only just. This Canada is a small hamlet, or possibly an extension of the village of Wellow, with which it is joined in a parish council but separated by the New Forest boundary. The nature of Canada is very different to Wellow. It is larger than West Wellow but has far fewer homes – all laid out in the rectangular pattern mentioned previously. Canada's homes are built for privacy, which is perhaps why such a small place needs three chapels and a pub. There is no snobbery, though: the 1908 Methodist chapel informs all and sundry it is a Primitive Methodist chapel.

Canada Common joins with West Wellow and Plaitford Commons to provide a lovely area for picnics, rambles, kite flying or dog walking. Numerous springs make the ground boggy in places and keep the ponies well watered. When it's time for human watering, the Rockingham Arms pub in the centre of Canada provides refreshments, a gift shop and an otherworldly piece of artwork in the garden.

S5 Tinney's Firs

GR SU 204197

One of the first things to note is the rectangular pond beside the car park. Neither is shown on the current OS map but they are both in the south-east corner of the wood and just inside the National Park boundary. The pond is easy to miss, but due to the reflection and any fallen leaves, it is a wonderful photo opportunity in all kinds of weather conditions. The shape of the pond indicates it is man-made.

The first stream you come to (also not shown) is unkempt, but in a good way. It's slow flowing, so fallen trees and even leaves can cause it to flood. In the winter it often resembles a series of cascades as it forces its way through a mass of oak, beech and birch leaf litter.

Fallen trees are generally left to rot so moss and fungus are common. 'Organised chaos' is the forestry term for it.

The tallest and most impressive trees are not in the woodland area but are the Douglas firs referred to in the name. Tinney's Firs are mostly on private land but, towering 50 metres above you, they are very obvious. Most of the rest of the woodland is deciduous and pleasant rather than stunning. However, good woodland management ensures that many species of butterfly and forest floor flowers thrive. Tinney's Firs is a great place to quickly access an area of woodland and escape from 'the world' for a while.

S6 Loosehanger Copse deer enclosure

GR SU 212188

In medieval times this was a deer park, but its name on an 1837 map, Loosehanger Park, reflects its enclosure in the 17th century. By the time of the OS 1 inch to 1 mile maps in the 1890s the name had changed to Loosehanger Copse, a fall from grace that perhaps reflected a change in the owner's circumstances.

The deer park's earth bank boundaries still surround most of Loosehanger Copse, and are particularly impressive examples. At its highest, the bank is over two metres tall, and at most points it is over a metre tall and two wide. Only the tallest person could see over it and this is after hundreds of years of erosion. Back in the day the bank would have been even more formidable.

It's a peaceful wood with the occasional bird sound, which could be a woodpecker's beak as well as a chirp or a cheep. Sparrowhawks and buzzards also regard the wood as home so the peace is occasionally disturbed by aerial shenanigans.

The damp, dark conditions of Loosehanger Copse are ideal for lichens and it is an SSSI for this reason. If you look closely you will see lichen proliferating all around you. Some lichen growth is on the relatively rare 700-year-old sessile oaks that have thrived here; younger examples can easily be spotted from the public right of way, towering above the towering earth bank.

S7 The gates of Hamptworth Lodge

GR SU 232193, 221196, 226198

Hamptworth Lodge is hidden behind thick clumps of rhododendron bushes and busy broadleaved woodland. This Tudor-style Edwardian house was built on a site occupied for hundreds of years by a grand Jacobean manor house. The only place where access is visible is where there are tracks. These tracks are guarded by all manner of gates.

At GR SU 226198 are two sets of gates, both very modern. One set leads past a gatehouse to the Lodge and, though new, they are flanked by the former gateposts. These stand over two metres tall and are what you would expect to find at a house of this status. The white-painted metalwork is ornate with swirls and squiggles. Designed by either a genius or a child, they are topped by a squiggled skewer, presumably to make life difficult for any wood pigeons wanting to settle. The second gate leads to the right of way travelling south west from the road. The gate is unremarkable.

The kissing gate at GR SU 221196 is far more impressive, though it has now fallen into disrepair and is bypassed. What the etiquette is for passing jammed kissing gates is unclear – be cautious who you walk with.

The pick of the crop are the two sets of gates at the crossroads of GR SU 232193. The southern gate is singular, with two sets of cross bracing and original white-painted steel gateposts. Opposite is a double gate, each with one set of cross bracing and substantial, modern wooden gateposts. An original metal gatepost still stands but is now redundant. In the past these gates would have been used by members of the household to access the New Forest via Nomansland or Franchises Wood.

S8 Hamptworth Hamlet

GR SU 244195

With the Cuckoo Inn at its heart, Hamptworth is everything you would expect of a hamlet. There is a sturdy farmhouse, neat cottages and a lot of thatched roofs alongside perfectly proportioned barns and brick sheds. There are sculpted yews, poplars stirring in the breeze and an oak tree giving shade to a bench. A shelter, a post box and a Millennium footpath map on a small plot of grass opposite the village duck pond are all further positives. However, all this would be as nought if the village pub was not shipshape and Bristol fashion, and the Cuckoo Inn does not disappoint. It is an 18th century thatched building in a large garden and surrounded by a wooden picket fence. The garden has covered areas, picnic benches for the summer and even a pétanque terrain.

The interior is just as appealing. The low ceilings create an intimate atmosphere and numerous rooms allow you to be sociable or not. There are log burners for the winter months. Curiosities include the pétanque spoon trophy (not wooden) and the locals.

Hamptworth is a great place to start a circular walk into the surrounding woodland, returning to the Cuckoo Inn for food and a pint.

T6 Drovers' roads

GR SU 223216

Part of a conversation in 2019 about drovers' roads in Wiltshire: 'My grandfather used to drive his flock of geese to Christmas market along a droveway,' said one current Wiltshire farmer. 'Mine bought a dining table at the market and carried it on his back all the way home along the same lane', replied a farmer's granddaughter.

Many drovers' roads were the medieval equivalents of motorways, used to move cattle from Wales to London for example. These droveways were wide, to allow large herds of cattle to be moved efficiently. The roads were abutted by hedges or earth banks; over centuries of use they often became sunken lanes. Professional drovers were highly regarded in the farming community, but during the 1800s trains began to transport livestock and the drovers' work gradually dwindled. More locally, droveways gave access to the nearest market towns. Droveways tended to have oak, beech and holly planted along the route to guide the drovers.

Much of the history of drovers and their routes has been lost but there are some clues locally. Stockbridge, to the north east of here, has a former drovers' inn with the Welsh inscription: 'GWAIR-TYM-HERUS-PORFA-FLASUS-CWRW-DA-A-GWAL-CYCURUS': 'Season's hay, rich grass, good ale and sound sleep'. Gussage All Saints in Dorset has a Drovers' Inn where pints are still poured. This drovers' road lies between the market town of Salisbury and the Royal Navy base in Portsmouth, which was a huge market for beef. It also runs close to Downton, a crossing on the River Avon. Many of the great trees that marked the route have been felled at this end of this lane but their stumps remain. Closer to Hamptworth Golf Course the trees are more impressive.

T7 Langley Wood National Nature Reserve

GR SU 227211

There are three entrances to Langley Wood but only one very small car park, at GR SU 219203. From any of the entrances you can follow a well-signposted triangular route that links the two main rights of way with a permissive path from GR SU 227211 to Round Copse corner. The path from the car park to the permissive path junction is very high quality and would allow wheelchairs and pushchairs access to the heart of the woodland.

Woodland management over many years has produced a bright and vibrant wood with an enormous variety of wildlife. Clearance of some trees has allowed grass, wood anemone and ferns to cover the floor and in the spring bluebells reign supreme. The trees that remain are glorious oak, alder, birch and small-leaved limes.

The key reason for this woodland being designated a National Nature Reserve is the bird life. Use this simple birding guide to spot some of the main species:

- Great spotted woodpecker – black and white with a red rear (2 points)
- Lesser spotted woodpecker – smaller and quieter than the 'Great'. A more obvious red head is typical (5 points)
- Green woodpecker – large and green with a red head. Loves to eat ants (3 points)
- Hawfinch – brown, white and black and large for a finch. Has a strong and obvious bill (5 points)
- Firecrest – tiny green, black and white bird. Constantly moving (3 points)
- Nuthatch – a chubby bird resembling a woodpecker. Grey on top with chestnut sides (2 points)
- Treecreeper – small and active bird with a thin, downturned beak. White belly and brown back (2 points)
- Robin – has a red breast! (1 point)
- Jay – large and colourful with a mix of cream, brown and black as well as blue on the wings (3 points)
- Nightingale – brown back gradually changing to white on front. Small but with a great song (4 points).

Any visit scoring more than 20 points must be regarded as highly successful. For more information on birding, try: www.rspb.org.uk/birds-and-wildlife/wildlife-guides/bird-a-z or a guidebook.

T8 Mushroom hunting in The Earldoms

GR SU 241212

The Earldoms is an area of private woodland with good access along public footpaths. Considerate parking is available along two stretches of minor road now bypassed by the A36. The area is a mix of woodland and farmland, so a walk here provides a real variety. Depending on your route, you can take in Redlynch Golf Course with its weeping willows, pampas grass and lily-filled water features. The remains of an Iron Age camp can provide a small distraction though they are almost hidden by undergrowth for most of the year.

During the autumn a plethora of mushrooms grow alongside the path running from Glazier's Copse to Bagfield Copse. As this is private land the mushrooms should not be picked but identifying them provides most of the fun anyway. Listed below are five of the most common and easy to identify mushrooms. Many more can be identified using a guidebook or online source.

- Common puffball (Lycoperdon perlatum). 2–5cm diameter, 3–8cm tall. A globular head that narrows to a wide stalk approximately halfway down. Young examples are white and have conical warts which fall off easily. Older examples are yellow to brown.
- Fleecy milk-cap (Lactarius vellereus). Cap 10–25cm, stem 4–10cm x 2–4cm. A convex cap with a funnel shape. Young examples are creamy white, becoming yellow/brown when mature. Damaged examples discolour and can exude a white milk.
- Hairy curtain crust (Stereum hirsutum). 2–6cm across, 2–3mm thick. Resembling wavy bacon crisps and frequently found on stumps, fallen trees and timber. Yellowy-orange fading to brown.
- Fawn mushroom (Pluteus cervinus). Cap 6–12cm, 4–10cm stem. Smooth brown cap sticking up in the centre. White to pink gills. Found on fallen wood, often surrounded by moss.
- Slimy milk-cap (Lactarius blennius). Cap 5–10cm, stem 4–5cm x 1–1.5cm. Found under beech trees (the Oak milk-cap is similar but found under oak!) Brown, grey and olive in colour. The cap is slightly depressed and shiny and slimy when wet.

U7 The Tsar's finger

GR SU 236222

There is a wonderful legend surrounding the building of the St Petersburg-Moscow railway during the reign of Nicholas I. In 1841, frustrated by a lack of progress on planning a route for the railway, Tsar Nicholas drew his own route. Eschewing curves and ignoring gradients, he took inspiration from the Romans and drew a straight line between the two cities using a ruler. Sadly, as many a school child knows, plans drawn in haste don't always work out. When the Russian ruler used his ruler to draw his line he bumped around his finger. The railway engineers had two choices: tell the Tsar he'd messed up and spend the rest of their days in Siberia, or build a perfectly straight railway with a digit-shaped deviation. Siberia is awfully cold in the winter so the legendary 'Tsar's finger' came into being.

Back to the New Forest: you'll note there are not too many long, straight lines. The roads and railway lines all tend to curve. There is a very odd finger-shaped extrusion in the north of the New Forest. In an area of generally straight field boundaries and footpaths someone has built a decidedly odd-shaped fence. Either that, or a cartographer has drawn around his whole finger in error or for fun. The latter possibility looks all the more feasible if you notice the four-finger pond just to the south. Looking every bit like a cold Bart Simpson's hand on the map, the real pond is much greener. Whilst the water is green, the woodland here is unattractive and the signage unfriendly. This is one of the few sites where the map is nicer than the reality.

U8 Northern exposure

GR SU 246229, 247228

When the New Forest became a National Park the park boundary was extended northwards into Wiltshire. There is a fair bit of forest in this area, such as Langley Wood National Nature Reserve, so it was a logical decision.

The northernmost part of the park lies just to the south of the delightful village of Whiteparish, on the A27. The village has a good shop and a couple of places to eat and drink. It also has an unusual church with a square spire. 600m south of the church lie the official and unofficial northern points of the New Forest.

I've declared official and unofficial northern points, rather in the manner of Queen Elizabeth II's birthdays, due to a kindly impulse on my part. To get to the official northernmost point your journey from Whiteparish church takes you down the road, past a school on the left and then past a track on the right. At the sixth house on the right you'll see a footpath sign on someone's outbuilding. The footpath takes you along this person's drive, past their car and right alongside their house. You get to walk through their back garden, possibly meeting them if they are having a barbecue or gardening, clamber over a stile in their back fence and then a second stile to achieve your objective. Your reward for all this intrusion is a view of a broken fence post, a stile and a bush. There is another route through some fields but the result is just as underwhelming.

The unofficial northernmost point is just a hundred metres further down the road at a Y junction. Here is a grassed area, suitable for a low-grade picnic, with a bus stop and views south of the official wooden 'New Forest' sign as well as a New Forest 40mph sign. A small area of woodland, the start of Whiteparish Common, is also visible and this is a far better place for a picnic.

Squares by subject

This section has been created to allow you to quickly reference topics of interest. It is not exhaustive, but indicative.

Trees

D11, D15, E4, E5, E11, E12, E13, E15, E16, F5, F7, F9, F10, F12, G4, G5, G6, G8, G9, G16, G17, G19, G20, G21, G22, H2, H5, H12, H13, H18, H21, I4, 15, I8, I9, I10, I11, I14, I15, I17, I19, J4, J7, J8, J9, J10, J11, J12, J17, K4, K6, K7, K8, K9, K11, K12, K16, L3, L5, L6, L7, L9, L10, L12, L13, L14, L15, L16, M4, M6, M8, M9, M10, M11, M12, M13, M14, N5, N8, N9, N10, N11, N12, O5, O6, O7, O8, O9, O10, O11, P3, P9, Q3, Q4, Q11, Q12, R4, R5, R6, R7, R8, R9, S5, S6, S7, S8, T6, T7, T8

Plants

C13, D11, D14, E11, E12, E13, E15, F14, F15, G4, G10, G12, G14, G17, G21, H4, H8, H9, I4, I7, I15, I17, I19, J4, J6, J12, J13, J14, J15, J16, K7, K12, K15, L4, L6, L13, L14, M4, M6, M11, M13, N3, N6, N9, O3, P4, R5, R6, R9, R10, S6, T8

Animals

C13, D11, D14, E7, E12, E13, F5, F8, F19, G4, G12, G14, G17, G21, G22, H4, H7, H8, H9, H17, H23, I4, 15, I7, I8, I10, I12, I15, I19, J4, J11, J12, J15, J17, K5, K8, K12, K13, K14, K15, K17, L4, L5, L6, L7, L8, L9, L10, L12, L13, L14, L16, M3, M4, M10, M11, M13, N6, N7, N9, N10, O4, O5, O6, O7, P11, Q2, Q4, Q10, R4, R5, R6, R9, R10, S5, S6, S7, T6, T7, T8

Villages

B12, E9, E11, F10, F12, F16, G18, H11, H12, H17, I6, I12, I22, L11, N10, N13, O12, O13, P10, P12, R3, R8, R11, S8, U8,

Pub/cafe

B12, D5, D13, E7, E11, E12, E15, E17, F8, F10, F12, F21, G7, G18, H11, H17, H23, I6, I17, I18, I19, I22, K14, L3, L10, L11, M5, N10, N13, O9, O13, P7, P10, P12, Q2, R3, R8, R11, S8, U8

Sport

E15, F11, G15, H19, H23, J7, L12, N12, Q12

Rivers/ponds

A12, B12, C13, D11, D13, E11, E13, E15, E16, F5, F9, F11, F15, F19, F20, G4, G10, G12, G14, G17, G18, G19, G20, G21, H1, H3, H4, H8, H9, H10, H11, H13, H15, H16, H17, H22, I4, I7, I8, I10, I11, I13, I14, I15, I16, I22, J8, J10, J14, J15, K3, K4, K12, K17, L4, L6, L7, L11, L14, M4, M6, M7, M11, M13, N6, N7, N9, N14, O5, O10, P6, P8, P10, Q2, Q3, R5, R10, S8

Coast

A12, B12, C13, D13, D14, D15, F19, F20, F21, F22, G22, H22, H23, I22

Historical site

A12, D13, E7, E10, E12, E15, F8, F10, F12, F13, F15, F16, F18, F21, G4, G5, G8, G16, G18, G19, G22, H2, H7, H12, H14, H17, H19, H23, 15, I6, I9, I11, I17, I18, I19, I22, J4, J5, J9, J13, J15, J16, J18, K3, K8, K9, K10, K12, K13, K15, L5, L12, L17, M10, M14, M15, N3, N7, N10, N11, O6, O9, O10, O11, P3, Q3, Q7, Q9, Q10, Q11, R3, R4, S7

Industrial heritage

C13, D5, D13, E7, E9, E11, E16, F11, F12, F18, G7, G9, G10, G11, G13, G17, H6, H15, H16, H22, I3, I11, I13, I14, I22, J7, K11, K14, K17, L3, L18, M5, M11, M12, M13, M16, M17, N5, R7, T6

Military

A12, D13, D15, E5, E12, E14, E15, F4, F6, F13, F17, F22, G15, G16, G18, H12, H13, H14, H18, H21, H23, I6, I12, I17, L9, L13, L15, L17, M3, M8, N8, O4, O7, O8, P5, P6, Q5, Q6, Q7, R8,

Cartography

E4, E13, E16, F7, F14, F15, F16, F19, G4, G9, G10, G11, G19, H1, H3, H4, H5, H6, H10, H15, I3, I10, I13, I15, I17, I18, J6, J13, K13, K17, N4, N11, O8, P8, Q8, U7, U8

Great for kids

A12, B12, C13, D15, E7, E11, E12, E15, F4, F6, F9, F11, F12, F14, F15, F19, F20, F21, F22, G9, G10, G12, G15, G18, G20, G22, H2, H3, H6, H9, H12, H13, H14, H15, H21, H23, I4, 15, I6, I7, I10, I11, I12, I13, I14, I17, I18, I19, I22, J4, J7, J8, J9, J12, J13, J14, J15, J18, K4, K6, K8, K9, K12, K15, K16, L3, L5, L7, L8, L9, L10, L12, L14, L16, M3, M4, M6, M9, M12, N3, N4, N5, N6, N7, N8, N9, N10, N11, N12, N14, O3, O4, O5, O6, O7, O8, O9, O11, O12, P4, P5, P6, P7, P8, P9, P10, Q2, Q3, Q5, Q8, Q9, Q10, R4, R5, R6, R7, R8, R9, R10, R11, S5, S6, S7, S8, T6, T7, T8

Seasonal

Spring

D14, F5, G12, G16, G17, G21, H8, H9, H12, H23, I4, I7, I8, I9, I19, J9, J11, J12, J15, K7, K12, K16, L8, L10, M4, M6, M7, M9, M11, M13, N6, N10, O5, O6, P4, Q2, R4, R5, R6, R9, R10, S6

Summer

B12, D13, D14, D15, E11, E15, F5, F8, F11, F12, F14, F19, F20, F21, F22, G4, G10, G12, G14, G18, G21, G22, H1, H2, H4, H8, H9, H12, H15, H17, H22, H23, I4, 15, I8, I9, I10, I11, I12, I14, I17, I19, I22, J4, J9, J10, J11, J12, J13, J14, J15, J18, K4, K6, K8, K9, K11, K12, K13, K14, K16, K17, L3, L4, L5, L6, L7, L8, L9, L10, L12, L13, L14, M3, M4, M5, M6, M8, M10, M13, M14, N3, N4, N5, N6, N8, N10, N12, N14, O3, O4, O5, O6, O7, O9, O10, O11, P3, P4, P5, P6, P7, P8, P9, Q2, Q3, Q4, Q5, Q6, Q8, Q10, Q11, Q12, R4, R5, R6, R7, R9, R10, S5, S6, S7, S8, T6, T7, T8

Autumn

D14, E15, F5, H8, H9, H11, H12, H23, I4, I8, I9, I15, I19, J9, J10, K6, K7, K9, K10, K11, K12, K13, K16, L5, L9, L10, M4, M8, M9, M11, M13, M14, N6, N8, N10, O4, O5, O6, O7, O9, O10, O11, P3, P4, P9, Q2, Q3, Q11, Q13, R4, R5, R6, R8, R9, S5, S6, S7, T6, T7, T8

Winter

E7, E11, F4, F8, G18, H11, H12, H17, H23, I6, I17, I22, J9, L17, M5, M9, M16, N6, N10, O5, P7, P10, P12, P13, Q2, Q9, R3, R11, S8

Additional information

This guidebook is not intended as an academic text so has not been footnoted in that manner. Direct quotes have been attributed on the relevant page. Any additional information has come from the following websites or publications.

https://historicengland.org.uk/

https://www.woodlandtrust.org.uk

https://www.newforestnpa.gov.uk/

http://trigpointing.uk/

https://www.salisburyjournal.co.uk

http://www.parkerseal.org.uk/articles/magazine/beaulieubeacon.aspx

https://beaulieuhistorysociety.org.uk/images/presentations/Beaulieu_River_Cruise/Beaulieu_River_Cruise.pdf

https://www.thecanterburyauctiongalleries.com/Lot/?sale=FA060218&lot=623&id=56911

http://www.southampton.ac.uk/~imw/New-Forest-Geology-Bibliography.htm#Small

http://www.wetroads.co.uk/hampshire.htm

https://metro.co.uk/2018/03/10/incredible-220-ft-tower-home-swimming-pool-set-raffled-off-just-10-7376731/

https://historicengland.org.uk/listing/the-list/list-entry/1302852

https://www.forestryengland.uk/blog/white-tailed-eagles-explore-the-isle-wight

https://www.bbc.co.uk/history/ww2peopleswar/timeline/factfiles/nonflash/a6650237.shtml

www.visionof Britain.org.uk/maps

www.newforestexplorersguide.co.uk

www.dailyecho.co.uk

www.advertiserandtimes.co.uk

https://www.newforestnpa.gov.uk/lidar/

https://nfknowledge.org/

'Hayward, J. (1991) Dartmoor 365: An Exploration of Every One of the 365 Square Miles in the Dartmoor National Park. Ottery St Mary: Curlew Publications.'

Answer to square E17 crossword:

Dire Straits members Mark Knopfler and John Illsley
and also billionaire Sir Jim Ratcliffe

Praise for
New Forest 222

Excellent book
Michael L G Couzins

Thoroughly enjoyed this book
Roger K

Fantastic little book, written by someone with a very good knowledge of the forest
David A P Smith

It's so nice to see a book that's written by someone who clearly loves the area, and knows so much about it
Ian Warner

I live very near to the New Forest and thought I knew it reasonably well until I read this!
Chris C

I have lived near the New Forest for 30 years now but this interesting book has revealed many new pieces of geography, history and ecology to me
John Tunney

Jodi proves that on any walk through the forest, you will find something of interest
Carol Flint, head of brand at the Ramblers

Notes

Notes

Notes

Notes

Notes

Notes

Notes

Notes

Notes

Notes

Notes